Gramsci and Media Literacy

Gramsci and Media Literacy

Critically Thinking about TV and the Movies

Erika Engstrom and Ralph Beliveau

LEXINGTON BOOKS

Lanham • Boulder • New York • London

Published by Lexington Books
An imprint of The Rowman & Littlefield Publishing Group, Inc.
4501 Forbes Boulevard, Suite 200, Lanham, Maryland 20706
www.rowman.com

6 Tinworth Street, London SE11 5AL, United Kingdom

British Library Cataloguing in Publication Information Available

Library of Congress Cataloging-in-Publication Data

Names: Engstrom, Erika, 1964- author. | Beliveau, Ralph, author.
Title: Gramsci and media literacy : critically thinking about TV and the movies / Erika Engstrom and Ralph Beliveau.
Description: Lanham : Lexington Books, 2021. | Includes bibliographical references and index.
Identifiers: LCCN 2021010408 (print) | LCCN 2021010409 (ebook) | ISBN 9781793619853 (cloth) | ISBN 9781793619860 (ebook)
Subjects: LCSH: Mass media—Political aspects. | Mass media—Social aspects. Gramsci, Antonio, 1891-1937. | Hegemony.
Classification: LCC P95.8 .E55 2021 (print) | LCC P95.8 (ebook) | DDC 302.23—dc23
LC record available at https://lccn.loc.gov/2021010408
LC ebook record available at https://lccn.loc.gov/2021010409

∞™ The paper used in this publication meets the minimum requirements of American National Standard for Information Sciences—Permanence of Paper for Printed Library Materials, ANSI/NISO Z39.48-1992.

Contents

1 Introduction 1

2 A Gramscian Approach to Media Literacy 27

3 Gramsci, Film, TV, and Cable Streaming: Toward Counterhegemony 49

4 Hegemonic Masculinity in the Mass Media 67

5 The Gendered *Endgame*: Marvel's New Man 85

6 Conclusion 111

Bibliography 121

Index 133

About the Authors 141

Chapter 1

Introduction

The year 2020 marked the time when an unprecedented series of events led to millions of people being forced to stay within the confines of their homes because of the spread of COVID-19, the disease caused by a novel coronavirus that would take a devastating toll. While healthcare workers and those considered essential to the functioning of the country served on the frontlines in the metaphorical battle with the virus, the population on the sidelines of that battle sought to contribute to the effort in their own ways. Ironically, even doing nothing became a way to do something. In the United States, it became somewhat of a joke that to do one's patriotic duty meant staying at home and binge-watching television, which, thanks to new technologies such as internet streaming services, demonstrated the ever-expanding abundance of mass-mediated content there for watching and re-watching. This content, in the form of television, film, podcasts, internet videos, talk shows, infotainment of all manner, and the reportage of events produced through the filter of news organizations that comprise an ever-shrinking number of transnational media corporations, serves as a reflection of the culture in which it is produced. Mass media, whatever their incarnations, offer a virtual, composite map of the cultural territories they represent.

In this book, we explore how mass media in the early decades of the twenty-first century serve as conduits for cultural ideologies—the ways in which people think about everyday life. Three key concepts guide our exploration: hegemony, media literacy, and semiotics. Hegemony is one of the significant contributions of Antonio Gramsci, a political philosopher who wrote about culture, ideology, and politics in the early decades of the twentieth century, to our understanding of the intertwining of culture and mass media. Hegemony refers to the unquestioned dominance of a social group, or configuration of social groups within a society, resulting from its ability

1

to maintain power indirectly through the implicit approval of non-dominant groups. Media literacy refers to the ability of media consumers to understand and identify the modes of media production and consider the purposes and meanings of media content. Semiotics refers to the study of the use of symbols—which include words, images, and their combinations—and the interpretation of those symbols. Throughout the chapters of this book, all three of these concepts guide our explanation of why Gramsci's thoughts on culture, media, and literacy continue to remain relevant to the study of mass media.

We approach our project through the lens of the writings of Gramsci, which continue to provide a means by which to analyze and explain how today's mass media help to keep cultural ideologies in place while simultaneously absorbing intrusions into those ideologies that challenge or threaten them. We examine how the discursive aspect of mass media content presents to audiences a portrayal of culture, that is, a "collective programming of the mind" (Hofstede, 1980, p. 13). In doing so, we invoke the tenets of media literacy as a means to uncover the ways in which media content can be read so as to peel back the veneer of entertaining narrative to reveal the ways in which ideas about social life become inculcated into the media we enjoy and sometimes offer models or reflections that speak to our own life experiences.

We aim here to point the way toward a deeper appreciation for critically approaching popular media by providing a series of contemporary analyses of the Gramscian theory of hegemony as applied to media content, processes, and forms. Specifically, we explore how dominant ideologies regarding education, gender and gendered practices, and media delivery in the contemporary U.S. mass communication environment become the commonsense viewpoints that maintain power structures and require the critical examination necessary for the progress toward an equitable, egalitarian society. We set out in this book to explore aspects of today's mass media armed with Gramscian media theory to address how cultural norms presented in media forms perpetuate notions of "common sense" consented to in everyday life while also seeing this as the battle between alternative explanations of the meanings of media experiences. In addition to using media literacy frames, in this book we use semiotics and the relationships between texts and critics as they struggle over the meanings of words, images, sounds, and stories that are produced, launched into the public sphere, discussed in the interactive space between mass media and social media, and confirmed in the actions that people take—or in some cases, do not take—as a way of expressing their acceptance or rejection of hegemonic meanings.

So why Gramsci? His role as a cultural theorist was critical to the development of cultural studies, which sought powerful ways to interpret meanings created by media culture that take into account a more active, participatory audience of viewers and to incorporate audience points of view into the media environment. Rather than being reduced to a mere feedback channel measured in ratings and dollars, the cultures of audiences would become a deeper and richer area of study through a more complex examination of the tension between consent and resistance that work within the theory of hegemony. And in the more recent media sphere, with the rise of interactive content, convergence cultures, fan communities, and social media, Gramsci's ideas become necessary when we critically examine the power relations between producers and audiences in an ever-increasingly complex media ecology.

To understand the contributions of Antonio Gramsci to the study of media and cultural production, we start first with describing who he was and how his theories provide an analytical tool for disentangling how cultural production, in the forms of mass media messages, incorporates dominant ideologies of society. The most prominent of Gramsci's theories is hegemony, a conception of the dynamic process in which emplaced structures of a culture resist change while absorbing alternatives to dominant ideology. We then turn to an explanation for how the study and analysis of mass media directly relate to Gramsci's notion of hegemony and the role of intellectuals as both arbiters of dominant thought and their potential to create critical awareness on the part of audiences.

Our goal for this book is to demonstrate that, as Gramsci asserted, anyone can be an intellectual and agent of change through media literacy and become culturally and critically aware citizens and even media creators who show that mass media can do so much more than just entertain or inform. Mass media also can educate, enlighten, and inspire all of us to participate in the creativity reflected in the articulation of meaning. Especially in an era when social media and legacy media interact with each other, hegemonic responses can go beyond the limits of ideological media construction, into areas of individual and collective debate over meaning. This can result in negative consequences due to the openness of the social media environment, leaving it vulnerable to intrusion by algorithmically driven software routines ("bots") and other means of exacerbating polarization. But it also holds the potential to draw on collective creativity, to share common desires for a better society, and to consolidate energy around issues that reflect expressions of the collective solidarity that also plays a part in the hegemonic process of the media.

GRAMSCI

"Antonio Gramsci is a name practically unknown in America, yet he is one of the leading thinkers of the last half century," wrote Marzani in his 1957 book *The Open Marxism of Antonio Gramsci* (p. 5). Antonio Gramsci (1891–1937) was a highly educated journalist and leader in the Italian Communist Party in the early 1920s; he was a political activist working on behalf of factory workers in the city of Turin. In Rome in 1926, just four years after the rise of the Fascist regime of Benito Mussolini, that regime imprisoned him for political reasons. In prison, he wrote down, in a series of notebooks, his thoughts about politics, culture, education, and, most relevant to this book, the intersection between the three. Gramsci himself, "one of the most prescient representatives of the Italian left," had predicted that unless people unified and took action against Mussolini during his rise to power in Italy's bleakness after World War I, "Italian democracy and Italian socialism would both suffer a disastrous defeat" (Rosengarten, n.d.). His intellect and influence as a force of resistance against the Fascist government cultivated what has become a symbol of his courage: a remark attributed to the public prosecutor who is said to have uttered about Gramsci when the Marxist was sentenced to prison: "For 20 years we must stop this brain from functioning" (Forgacs, 2016, p. 353).

Born in Sardinia, Gramsci came from a large family headed by a father who was a local civil bureaucrat (Hoare and Sperber, 2016). This class position came crashing down, however, when Antonio's father was thrown into prison, accused of embezzlement in 1897, when Antonio was six. The family's financial situation was devastated, though his mother worked hard to support the seven children. By the time of his father's release from prison in 1904, their plight was desperate. Antonio Gramsci also started to show signs of a spinal malformation thought to be due to Pott's disease, a variant of tuberculosis, which led to physical suffering through a crooked spine. As a result, as a young person, Antonio was experiencing both material and physical challenges that certainly helped to shape the thinker he would become. He had suffered teasing and bullying from other kids who called him *Antonu su gobbu* ("Antonio the hunchback"). After his father's release from prison, Antonio was able to stop working just to support the family and was able to return to school. In 1908 he moved in with his older brother Gennaro, who had already started thinking as a militant supporter of socialist ideas and actions. Thus, Antonio Gramsci's interest in socialism early on is attributable to the way one of his older brothers embraced the philosophy (Rosengarten, n.d.). It also reflected what he learned from his challenging cultural and physiological experiences. Being from the southern part of a still-fractured Italy, he experienced the bigotry reflected by perceptions of difference between the higher-status north and the poorer south, which was considered culturally inferior.

In 1911, Gramsci earned a scholarship to the University of Turin, where he took courses across a range of subjects, particularly the humanities and linguistics. In tracing the roots of Gramsci's take on cultural differences between groups under an overall "national" culture, especially disparities between regions and of class, Martin (2002) explained how Gramsci's own experiences as a Sardinian served as an example of those disparities. The majority of people in Italy spoke regional dialects, rather than the "official" Italian language representative of the country as a whole; this was true until after World War II. As a Sardinian, Gramsci spoke the Sardi dialect, and had to learn "real" Italian in addition to the version he learned first. "To study linguistics, therefore, was to be aware of the social and cultural unevenness of the Italian nation and of the gap between its official, political form and the lives and experiences of ordinary people" (p. 2). Gramsci's astute and keen awareness of the developmental unevenness that marked Italy's north and south, with the south at a disadvantage, coupled with differences in language use, marks just one of the bases upon which he built his work.

Gramsci joined the *Partito Socialista Italiano* (Italian Socialist Party) in 1912 and began working as a journalist a couple of years later. Newspapers were typically connected with political parties in Europe in this era, at a time when U.S. newspapers were coming out of a phase of yellow journalism and heading into the tabloid press, driven by selling papers as goods that offered sensationalism. Gramsci's work at *Il Grido del Popolo* starting in 1915, and its commitment to socialist politics, led to his setting up *L'Ordine Nuovo*, a weekly review of socialist culture, in 1919. He became a delegate for the Italian Socialist party in 1922 and lived in Moscow from May 1922 to November 1923. Throughout this time the development of the Italian Fascist party was underway, and many of the activists on the left saw it as a desperate expression of failing property-owning classes (Hoare & Sperber, 2016).

Gramsci was elected to the Chamber of Deputies, the lower house of the Italian Parliament in April 1924, which would have given him immunity from arrest. He returned to Italy in May of that year. But the Fascists under Mussolini outlawed Gramsci's party and he was arrested in November 1926. He spent the next decade in prison, where he wrote the series of notebooks that came to be the most influential part of his intellectual legacy. Unfortunately, his health deteriorated gradually during his time in prison, which failed to offer adequate care. Over the last few years of his life he was too weak to read and write. He was transferred to a clinic in Rome in 1935 but never regained his health and died in April 1937. He was forty-six.

As a political philosopher, Gramsci's primary focus centered on explaining and addressing the reasons why European socialist movements, like the one in which he was involved in Italy, failed as opposed to the success of the Russian Revolution (Carragee, 1993; Holub, 1992; Martin, 2002). One must ground this work and consider it within the historical context of the wake of World War I and the economic devastation it wrought as well as in terms of revisions in national identity that followed. Approaching this question required a rethinking of Marxism and the conditions required for radical and revolutionary change, and in doing so Gramsci "critically confronted the fact that the economic crisis situation in the various Western countries had not led to political crisis, as Marx had predicted," explained Holub (1992). "Rather, power and authority were still retained by the state and capitalism, in spite of the massive social and ideological upheavals currently taking place" in the 1920s and 1930s (p. 5).

Gramsci had married and was the father of two children, the younger of whom he never met. After his death in 1937, Gramsci's notebooks eventually became published and became known as *The Prison Notebooks*. They consisted of thirty-three writing exercise books containing a smattering of "notes, drafts, jottings, and some translations," which were preserved by his sister-in-law, Tatiana Schuct (Buttigieg, 1986, p. 2). She was pivotal in ensuring Gramsci's notebooks eventually became published. In 1948, they were published, in what was to become a classic in social theory of the twentieth century (Thomas, 2009). Although the historical context and particulars of the social and political situations of the time in which Gramsci lived necessarily contextualize what he wrote about, Gramsci provided a new language with which to approach the understanding and processes of politics and social phenomena in a broader context—and the tools to understand those processes a century later (Schwarzmantel, 2015).

The contents of the notebooks reflected Gramsci's exploration of a wide array of topics covering not just politics and a critical analysis of Marxism, but history, philosophy, cultural and literary criticism, and educational theory and practice. The intertwining of education with his lived experiences played an immensely important role in Gramsci's purpose as a proponent of social change that underpinned his life's work (Buttigieg, 2002). McNally (2015) described *The Prison Notebooks*, written between 1929 and 1935, as surpassing all of Gramsci's efforts prior to those many years in prison and "secured him a privileged place in the canon of twentieth-century Marxist thought" (p. 4), a conclusion similar to Buttigieg's (2002) assessment that Gramsci was "perhaps the most original Marxist thinker of his generation" (p. 67). His significant contribution to the understanding and critical assessment of Marxist theory serves as the impetus for an entire line of inquiry in political theory. However, Martin (2015) observed that a more accurate way of framing Gramsci's status would be to see him as a "theorist of the transition between social orders rather than an analyst of contemporary capitalism" (p. 48).

Santucci (2010) noted that books on Gramsci numbered in the hundreds and essays in the thousands, and by 1986 Gramsci was "one of the 250 most frequently cited authors in arts and humanities literature worldwide" (p. 27).[1] Although Gramsci thought and wrote about the times and events he witnessed in a particular historical moment, his ideas remain timeless and relevant a century later. Schwarzmantel (2015) described Gramsci's *Notebooks* as a classic text of the last century's political thought that continues to offer us a path to answering Gramsci's central question: "How can a process of moral and intellectual reform be initiated and carried to a successful conclusion?" (p. 292).

The Prison Notebooks may hold the answer, but this quest relies on the ability to piece together the scattered clues Gramsci left for us, much like breadcrumbs through the forest, because "his thoughts are not arranged in logical sequences and organic wholes; nowhere are his ideas systematically expounded" (Femia, 2002, p. 264). One can find a plethora of descriptors for the writings of Antonio Gramsci as presented in this classic text, including fragmentary, dispersed, partial, unfinished, provisional, incomplete, unsystematic, exploratory, unedited, and difficult to interpret because Gramsci often had to write using code words so as to elude the censorship of his captors (Bates, 2002; Femia, 2002; Hobsbawm, 1982; Kenway, 2001; Mouffe, 2002; Mumby, 1997; Williams, 2002). More reflective than his earlier writings as a militant journalist, Femia (2002) explained that the disjointed nature of the *Notebooks* came from the fact that Gramsci wrote down ideas for future study rather than fully explicated essays or research, and posed questions which he answered with possible solutions. Given these parameters, cautioned Buttigieg (1986), "there exists no point of arrival" when analyzing Gramsci's work (p. 15). Although one may read what Gramsci wrote incorrectly, neither does there exist a definitive, correct interpretation. And much of what we can glean from his writings depends on the work of subsequent Gramscian scholars, whose interpretations, insights, and applications of those disjointed notes help us to understand how the media industry as a whole and as a component of civil society exerts indirect power that upholds the state apparatus. This is precisely why we rely on secondary sources to understand the nuances inherent in taking what Gramsci wrote nearly a century ago in a time when mass communication existed in different, yet sometimes similar, forms as they do today.

However problematic or incomplete and open to myriad interpretations and conclusions, Gramsci's work presented in the *Notebooks* does offer several theoretical springboards we can use to explain the imperviousness to social change and ways to overcome it. This harkens back to Gramsci's underlying question of how to initiate reform and see it to conclusion: "In seeking to explain the failure of European socialist movements in the early twentieth century, Gramsci argued that capitalistic societies were sustained not only by the formal and potentially coercive power of the state, but also by complex cultural and ideological processes that secure popular consent to the established order" (Carragee, 1993, p. 330). In short, in those places where socialist movements failed, there existed something besides the power of the state that prevented reform and change from occurring in the wider society. Gramsci pondered the source of that something: *egemonia*, or hegemony.[2] Femia (2002) and Martin (2002) characterized hegemony as the unifying theme running throughout Gramsci's writings. Broadly defined, it refers to "a situation wherein a social group or class is ideologically dominant" (Femia, 2002, p. 264). This rough conception of hegemony serves as the starting point for exploring the ongoing influence of Gramsci, his theories, his goals, and their relevance to media literacy today.

HEGEMONY

Gramsci sought to discover how power works on a macro-level scale; this wide-angle view considers two main spheres that exert that power either directly or indirectly via *dominio*, or domination, and *egemonia*, or hegemony (Landy, 1986). Gramsci specified how a society becomes organized and functions through the way power becomes enforced on two levels: civil society and the state: "These two levels correspond on the one hand to the function of 'hegemony' which the dominant group exercised throughout society and on the other hand to that of 'direct domination' or command exercised through the State and 'juridical' government" (Gramsci, 1971, p. 145). Domination relates to the power of the state, while hegemony concerns civil society. The state refers to "political society," and its power becomes enforced through laws and government. Gramsci further defined civil society as the "ensembles of organisms commonly called 'private'" (p. 145).

Civil society, explained Mumby (1997), comprises the fabric of society that interweaves aspects of everyday life, such as the education system, religion, the family, and mass media. Hegemony "involves the production of a worldview, inclusive of a philosophical and moral outlook" that allied groups within civil society actively support (p. 48). Allied here means that they do not conflict with each other but function in such a way as to keep society running smoothly, what Lewis (1992) called a "terrain of ideology" (p. 280). Within the framework of Gramsci's thoughts on why socialist movements failed in capitalistic systems, cohesion (and thus resistance to radical social change) "depends primarily on the hegemony, that is, the spiritual and cultural supremacy of the ruling class, which through manipulation of civil society . . . manages to instill its values and beliefs on the rest of the population" (Femia, 2010, p. 570).

The worldview created from the values and beliefs supported by the ruling class—an amalgam of the civil institutions that exert influence—does not impose or enforce itself the way the state imposes its force through its legal power. Gramsci explained that people give status and authority to social institutions, rather than allowing that status and authority to be forced upon them: "The 'spontaneous' consent given by the great masses of the population to the general direction imposed on social life by the dominant fundamental group;

this control is 'historically' caused by prestige (and consequent confidence) which the dominant group enjoys because of its position and function in the world of production" (Gramsci, 1999, p. 145).[3] Gitlin (1987) interpreted this dominance as not necessarily meaning that a single group holds prestige or earns the confidence of those outside those social institutions influencing the ways in which social life functions. Rather, it is "best understood as a collaborative process rather than an imposed, definitively structured order" (p. 241).

In the Gramscian view, the dominant social groups (or elite) share social, economic, and cultural positions and norms. The prestige they hold originates from their collective power and control over the production of ideas, in addition to their direct or indirect influence on the state and its varying related institutions, like the education system and the media. By controlling the production of ideas, the dominant groups have the ability to silence and marginalize alternative ways of thinking, thus retaining their influence.

This becomes even more relevant to the study of mass media, in that this prestige becomes wielded through the institutions of civil society—conceived of as being organized and holding some degree of authority—that have control over the production of ideas which may not collude with each other directly, but nevertheless reinforce commonly held beliefs and values between each other. For example, if a culture upholds the nuclear family as the most common and most correct form of a family, we are taught this in school by reading stories in which nuclear families are the most common to appear. We learn from observation and experience that weddings are usually held in a church and consist of a man and a woman getting married and who eventually have their babies christened in church, and we see portrayals of the nuclear family on television and in movies. The familiar and "normal" ways that life unfolds for most people become hegemonic because they are not questioned—and are thus given consent *because* they are not questioned. In other words, hegemony exists as a "silent domination that is not experienced as domination at all" (Gitlin, 1987, p. 241). And like much of what happens in rituals, it becomes thoroughly normalized, while at the same time being de-historicized; it is experienced as if it has always been thus.

This unconscious domination, then, allows power in the form of civil society to rule by *ideas* rather than force (Bates, 2002). Alternative ideas may be held by a large number of people, but if they lack access to educational and media organizations—the ones who disseminate the prestige groups' perspectives and version of the wider world—those ideas cannot reach the wider population. Even when political and social protests gain the attention of the media, the views expressed by the protesters often become framed as out of the norm: the very fact that people have to break with their normal routines to take to the streets enhances the extraordinariness of their views. Hence, hegemony manages to imbue those "normal" and accepted viewpoints originating from the dominant social groups into civil society. What the state controls through regulations and governance, civil society promotes through the normalization and validation of practices dictated by the state. When considering how Gramsci categorized sources of power as direct and indirect, Holub (1992) summarized it this way: "If political society potentially disciplined the bodies, civil society disciplined above all the mind" (p. 197).

Culture—the totality of a group's way of life and the shared "programming of the mind"—serves as the site at which the struggle between dominant ideology and opposition and resistance occurs in civil society.[4] Mercer (1979) cautioned that culture is not imposed, nor does it spontaneously emerge from a pure class. Representations of the hegemonic order, of dominant ideologies within a culture and those common among cultures, appear in forms of cultural production. These include stage plays, songs, literature, fashion, video games, and any form of artistic expression, really. Mass communication—in the forms of television, film, music, newspapers, and so on—conveys ideology as well, and together these messages "saturate the average citizen" with meanings that may reflect the material experiences of most people but are ultimately produced by those who control the means of production (Zompetti, 2012, p. 368).[5]

The consensual struggle for dominancy described by Day (2005) in the context of global relationships between nation-states applies to struggles for dominancy within a culture as well: "It is crucial to note that hegemony is a process, not an accomplishment, that the actions of a dominant group are always open to contestation" (p. 7).

Incorporated into the control over the means of production is control over the forces of *reproduction* as well. Education systems and the powers that they impose have an outward appearance of being more functional than political. But they also serve as the main proponents of the way civil society operates. History and civics education creates a web of meanings that provide continuity to the hegemonic order. Apple (1979) described this as "official knowledge":

> Schools do not only control people; they also help control meaning. Since they preserve and distribute what is perceived to be "legitimate knowledge"—the knowledge that "we all must have," schools confer cultural legitimacy on the knowledge of specific groups. But this is not all, for the ability of a group to make its knowledge into "knowledge for all" is related to that group's power in the larger political and economic arena. Power and culture, then, need to be seen, not as static entities with no connection to each other, but as attributes of existing economic relations in a society. They are dialectically interwoven so that economic power and control is interconnected with cultural power and control. (pp. 63–64)

In civil society, hegemony coordinates education with culture expressed through media, as well as with museums, information systems, official representations and commemoration of history, and the normalization of hierarchies of culture in terms of gender, race, class, and other identity markers.

Culture itself does not follow "laws"—although political society certainly can reflect the values of civil society—that are enforceable the way the state enforces the laws of the government. Rather, its indirect control is exerted through customs, practices, and attitudes that hold the status of "common sense," what everyone already knows. Gramsci defined common sense (*senso comune*) as "the conception of the world which is uncritically absorbed by the various social and cultural environments in which the moral individuality of the common [person] is developed" (Gramsci, 1999, p. 343).[6] As conventional wisdom, common sense unifies groups and societies into cultural formations; the following of common sense gives people not only something in common but also leads to an uncritical acceptance of beliefs, norms, and values (Zompetti, 1997).

In Western cultures today, for example, marriage is associated with a schema, or pattern, of which a formal marker is the wedding, which everyone "knows" requires certain rituals and material items used in patterned ways (a ceremony with guests wherein the marrying couple recite vows to each other while wearing special, formal clothing for the occasion, for example). However, even with common practices, there always exists the possibility that a couple may not follow the familiar procedure; they may elope instead, foregoing the expected intricacies associated with weddings that have become familiar within these cultures because of personal experiences with other weddings or seeing weddings depicted in magazines, television shows, or movies. There is no enforceable law prohibiting alternatives to the traditional wedding, but weddings that do not follow the familiar pattern may be met with skepticism, disappointment, or disapproval by those who endorse the accepted, expected traditional version. And a couple may stay together for years, even decades, without ever marrying—in opposition to the accepted way that commitment is expressed, or expected to be expressed, in a certain society. In addition, in the US, not until 2015 were married same-sex couples ruled to be entitled to equal treatment under the law, further evidence of how hegemonic thought within civil society was privileged and enforced via the state.

When one takes into consideration a "meta" way of thinking of all the state and civil apparatuses that maintain certain ways of thinking, of living, and of learning about the norms and expected behaviors in a society, the combination of ideological structures—the state, education, established religion (the Church), the press and mass media industries—poses a huge obstacle to not only the dissemination of new ideas but also to a revised worldview. Gramsci posed a central question that thus undergirds our purpose in writing this book:

"What resources can an innovative class set against this formidable complex of trenches and fortifications of the dominant class?" (Gramsci, 2000, p. 381).

Gramsci called common sense "the philosophy of non-philosophers" (Gramsci, 2000, p. 343). What Gramsci called good sense, on the other hand, refers to empirical knowledge: while a practice or belief may be commonsensical, it does not mean it is always valid or correct, while good sense results when common sense is "imbued with knowledge and reason" (Lears, 1985, p. 59). If the common sense associated with weddings means spending lots of money, and a couple sees such expenditure as not being good sense, then they may reject the traditional version of a wedding for something else. When alternatives—or counterhegemonies—to the "regular" way of doing things reach a critical mass, and become so widespread, accepted, and normalized to the point that what once just yesterday was thought of as the "right" way becomes thought of as "old fashioned," a revised hegemony is formed. This process does not happen overnight, and Gramsci's ideas about social change and the reasons why it happens, why it might happen slowly, or why it may not happen at all help to explain it.

The potential for counterhegemony serves as an important caveat to the hypothesized way that hegemony as indirect power works. Within the realm of civil society, hegemony does not operate in a monolithic, all-encompassing way. Gramsci's bird's eye view of hegemony does not portray a closed or static system. Rather, "it is a society in constant process where the creation of counterhegemonies remains a live option" (Lears, 1985, p. 571). Simply put, as feminist media scholar Linda Steiner described it, hegemony is always "leaking."[7] The normalization of certain values in a culture thus functions in terms of an equilibrium, a state of flux that involves what Williams (2002) identified as a continual process of "persuasion, consent, and consolidation" (p. 233). Dominant viewpoints always are challenged in some form by alternative ways of thinking. Gramsci believed in the "power of the reflective human subject," noted Femia (2010, p. 568). This belief in the agency of individuals and creativity in human action served as the foundation for his writings. Even as the totality of beliefs, attitudes, and practices may hold sway in the form of dominant ideology, the undercurrent of counter-ideologies and counterhegemonies always remains present. Numerous academic disciplines refer to Gramsci's articulation of hegemony, such as history, social movements, international relations, social and political theory, sociology, critical geography, anthropology, nursing, literary studies, and several that we directly address in this book, specifically, cultural studies, media studies, education studies, and feminism.[8]

For change to occur, however, alternative ways of thinking and doing need to come from within the existing culture itself. As Sassoon (1987) summarized, "An alternative hegemony and alternative structures are only possible historically . . . if they are based on embryonic ideas, practices and institutions which are already in evidence in the lives of the vast majority" (p. 20). Sassoon further touched on the tendency for people within a society or culture to always be challenging conventional thought, already living outside the parameters of acceptability that the ruling coalition of social institutions still indirectly and "softly" impose. "Gramsci suggests, in fact, that the material circumstances of the mass of the population are often historically 'ahead' of both the popular and dominant ideas" (p. 20). In other words, the "rules" that govern civil society are usually behind what's really going on in most people's lives. Eventually, the two will "catch up" to each other—resulting in social change that becomes the new dominant ideology. Though continual, this cycle may take longer than the type of change sought by Gramsci and the sociopolitical movement for which he worked so hard to see realized.

Critical thinking and the ability to deconstruct and question the taken-for-granted power and functions of state and civil institutions become vital to that realization of the just and equitable world Gramsci envisioned. It is by simply starting to question the unquestioned that true change begins. Much like bumper stickers that tell us to "QUESTION AUTHORITY," the Gramscian perspective guides the critical thinker along the path toward thinking for ourselves—and accepting alternatives to what we had believed (or thought we believed). Gramsci specifically wrote about the acceptance of otherwise hidden worldviews as a way to begin the transformation of society: "When an individual from the masses succeeds in criticizing and going beyond common sense, [that individual] by this very fact accepts a new philosophy" (Gramsci, 2000, p. 345). Herein lies the promise of hegemony as a theory for social change, as explained by Mouffe (2002): "The creation of a new hegemony . . . implies the transformation of the previous ideological terrain and the creation of a new world view which will serve as a unifying principle for a new collective will" (p. 306). Thus the cycle begins anew, as that new collective programming of the mind meets inevitable resistance, which in turn and in time becomes hegemonic, and so on.

HEGEMONY AND MASS MEDIA

The theory of hegemony sets out to explain why things stay the same and how things can change. Zompetti (1997) explained that Gramsci perceived hegemony as a "discursive creation," the product of "ensembles of power formed by cultural presentations, including rhetoric" (p. 73). In other words, hegemony occurs through *communication*. Analyses of mass media enlist this analytical tool that Gramsci left as a legacy in his search to understanding the challenges of societal reformation and re-formation. Gramsci constantly asked why people accepted certain ideas, and premised that those ideas somehow reflect the material, lived conditions of "real life"—which combine to give those ideas validity (Sassoon, 1987). For Gramsci, emplacement of cultural worldviews occurs from our perceptions, which rely to an extent on constructs built from social interaction and our ideas about how we should behave, think, and feel. This, argued Femia (2010), serves as the foundation for Gramsci's reputation as a theorist.

Mass media, as previously mentioned, serve as a collective site that provides and selectively constructs "social knowledge" (Hall, 1977, pp. 340–341). Through images and words, media messages not only cultivate cultural ideology, but they serve as means by which dominant ideologies within cultures become communicated so as to make them normal, natural, and a conduit of indirect control in civil society. "The press," wrote Gramsci (1999), "is the most dynamic part of this ideological structure, but not the only one. Everything which influences or is able to influence public opinion directly or indirectly belongs to it" (p. 380). Gramsci became prominent as a political leader but worked as a journalist up to the time of his arrest; he saw himself not as a professional journalist but considered his role as one aiming to build a new kind of society (Santucci, 2010). In addition to his militant journalism on behalf of the socialist cause, Gramsci wrote reviews of plays, which Dombroski (1986) argued demonstrated Gramsci's awareness that drama and the content of plays (and, today, film and television) could influence audiences by not just reinforcing dominant ideology, but also challenging and subverting it.

Recognizing that cultural production "is integrally linked to political and economic considerations," Gramsci was interested in a wide range of cultural production, including literary forms; these included "modernist writing, detective novels, Gothic romances, novels of intrigue, science fiction, and cinema," with discussions of various media forms "interrogative rather than prescriptive," noted Landy (1986, p. 61). However, he wrote very little in the way of specifically discussing emerging media of his time, such as radio and cinema, except for how he saw cinema as replacing the theatre and how film could convey meaning solely through images (Landy, 2008).[9] Even so, Gramsci acknowledged the power of new modes of mass communication and the need to understand their role as purveyors of culture in capitalistic systems (Landy, 1994). Briziarelli and Karikari (2016) asserted that Gramsci saw journalism and popular literature as crucial when considering the struggle between the maintenance of dominant ideology and alternatives to it. Indeed, they pointed out, Gramsci argued for a more aggressive journalism that exposed oppression across society, even when that oppression did not directly affect the working class. Today, we use hegemony theory and Gramsci's ideas about cultural production to examine all forms of communication that serve this function. "Mass media," used in the singular sense, serves as a starting point for analyzing exactly what kinds of ideologies are communicated through various modes, which serve as what Gitlin (1980) called "core systems" for distributing ideology.

Under capitalism, mass media exist to make money, and, implicit to their survival, they cannot afford, literally, to offer a product that their audiences may reject. "Mass media" here means commercial mass media. Hence, as Kellner (2009) pointed out, the production of culture (via media forms) and its distribution are implicitly profit oriented. Gitlin (1987) argued that the "genius" of the culture industry—that is, mass media—lies in its ability to package values and conflicts that may occur because counterhegemonic values are always possible; the media present them in terms that are compatible with dominant ideologies. However, there remains the potential for infusing media messages with just enough "new" thought already present in the culture. When considered within the Gramscian frame of civil society, mass media also play a role in the interconnectedness of influence and power that exists between the other components of civil society, which all indirectly connect to the state. Above this, however, lies the economic element of mass media, which, cyclically, also connects to the state not only in terms of upholding the economic system endorsed by the state, but also the ideas of the state that are validated by civil society. Gramsci recognized the intertwining of economic, political, and social institutions, noting "for though hegemony is ethico-political, it must also be economic, must necessarily be based on the decisive function exercised by the leading group in the decisive nucleus of economic activity" (Gramsci, 1971, p. 161). In this manner, it is in the best interest of commercial media, then, to uphold hegemonic thought in order to stay in business: to challenge the status quo becomes an economic gamble.

As a component of civil society, then, commercial mass media play a role in the hegemonic process, sometimes deliberately (such as in advertising), overtly (such as political messages), and obtusely (such as in films whose overtly obvious narratives disguise a deeper sociopolitical theme), as we will show in the chapters of this book. Overshadowing all of this remains market considerations of capitalism, which bind the parameters of what Artz (2018) termed "cultural creativity": distributors and producers of films, television, and other media make their choices not because of their artistry but based on the size of the audience they will attract and the amount they can charge advertisers (p. 5). This is especially true for transnational media, who strategize on how to best make a return on their investment and make their products appealing across cultures. The result then becomes cultural hegemony—by which one or a handful of dominant ideologies become asserted over others.

Media content can either uphold an ideology that enjoys the status of dominance or can be used in a strategic fashion that counters hegemonic thought, and thus holds the potential that Gramsci saw in the power of mass communication. An aspect of Gramsci's work focused on the ideology present in popular culture, which originates from the "people" (Storey, 2009). In this sense, forms of popular culture—as opposed to "high culture," which refers to the fine arts—reflect the authentic culture of the people, explained Storey. Gramsci didn't see culture in terms of high or low: both hold equal dignity (Pagano, 2017). He was interested in popular culture because, Forgacs (2000) explained in *The Antonio Gramsci Reader*, it was "bound up with his conception of revolutionary change as a process in which popular mentalities and behaviour are transformed" (p. 363). Thus, the theory of hegemony relies on "cultural" rather than economic data for explaining why socialism and the socialist movement that Gramsci fought for failed, a result of not only the failings of leadership within the movement but an inability to gain access to the production and distribution of their message through the commercial mass media.

Herein lies the same dilemma and challenge faced by activists today: the ownership and physical production of media messages are held in the hands of an increasingly smaller number of media organizations who have the equipment and manpower (literally) to create cultural products that continue to uphold the status quo, the hegemony resultant of civil society's support of and for the state. Hegemony explains why media messages that contain certain viewpoints are so familiar and already known that we do not even realize or question where and how they originate, or who benefits from the conveyance of those viewpoints. Those viewpoints, repeatedly sent and which add to our understanding of what is acceptable, unacceptable, or possible to change, encompass ideas about gender, education, and even how mass media operate as conduits of meaning among members of a culture, be it national or regional, between cultures and nations, and across the world.

CRITICAL AWARENESS

Gramsci was greatly concerned with education. Indeed, as Pizzolato and Holst (2017) stated, education "stands at the core of the theoretical architecture of his opus" (p. 1). Gramsci saw schools and education systems as getting students ready for the existing social order (Schwarzmantel, 2015). He considered education the key to social change and wrote at length about what it means to be a thinking person and the purpose of thinking in and of itself. He asked if it was better to think "without having a critical awareness" and take part in a conception of the world imposed on oneself by the external environment and the groups to which one automatically belongs, or if it was better to work out "consciously and critically" one's own conception of the world (Gramsci, 1999, p. 626). In other words, should we just go along, unaware of the ways in which our ideas of the world are created by others, or should we think for ourselves, critically and thoughtfully? The answer, Gramsci believed, is the latter.

Critical awareness serves as a vital part of a collective effort to instigate change, and it starts at the level of the individual. Bates (2002) explained that Gramsci saw questioning common sense and the status quo as a prerequisite to social change: "To achieve a revolutionary perspective, the worker must first be freed of the ideological fetters imposed on him by the cultural organizations of the ruling class"; this happens through critically understanding oneself, and the "awareness of being part of a definite hegemonic force" (p. 253). The combination of self-awareness and awareness of the ways in which cultural meanings are created, and what they tell us about what to think and how to behave, provides the key to Gramsci's focus not only regarding education but in answering the question of what explains resistance to the transformation of a society.

Bates (2002) noted that "hegemonic struggle requires the leadership of intellectuals" (p. 253). Gramsci wrote a great deal on intellectuals; he expanded the conception of intellectuals based on situational factors (such as rural and urban), noting that, really, all people basically possess a "certain number of qualifications of an intellectual nature," with their role in society not determined by those things, but by the social relations which characterize their position (Gramsci, 2000, p. 304). In essence, everyone is an intellectual, but being an "intellectual" is not their main occupation.[10] Sassoon (1982) explained that Gramsci, when he considered what an intellectual—as an occupation—does, used the term "intellectual" to describe "all those people who have an organizational or ideological-cultural role in society," such as teachers, civil servants, social workers, and journalists (p. 14). For the purposes of the argument we offer here, this group ought to include the producers of media culture, from the writers, actors, and directors of film and television, to the technical engineers who produce and maintain algorithms and the World Wide Web, to the participants in social media who both create and critique, who both construct and destroy. The term "culture producers" may more accurately reflect the intellectual role performed by all those involved in the process of creating any message sent through media channels, whether media industries in the economic sense or those who upload content through social media outlets.

The concept of the intellectual as applied to the creation of thought and ideology, however, becomes enhanced when one considers the hegemonic struggle of cultural production. As Femia (2010) pointed out, "Gramsci's preoccupation with the battle of ideas encouraged him to analyze the role of intellectuals in shaping mass psychology" (p. 517). Intellectuals specialize in idea formulation and dissemination, noted Harris (2015), and do not always do so conspiratorially; they may do it unconsciously. In particular, Gramsci identified two categories of intellectuals to describe those who participate in this endeavor in some way: traditional intellectuals, whose function derives from earlier times periods and who think of themselves as being "above" struggles of economics and politics (such as scholars, artists, and even priests); and organic intellectuals, whose work reproduces a particular society and who "organically" arise from the social groups they belong to, represent, and therefore are more closely tied to (such as civil servants, political activists, managers).[11] Although organic intellectuals aren't typically perceived as intellectuals in the usual sense, they engage just like traditional intellectuals in "the propagation of values and attitudes that either sustain or undermine the established order" (Femia, 2010, p. 571). As Gitlin (1987) explained, organic intellectuals include "skilled groups of symbolic adepts" upon whom corporate and political elites depend; these include media workers—journalists, producers, writers, actors, and everyone who works in mass media—because as cultural practitioners they are involved in integrating ideas and understandings in the interests of and between elites (those in power) and between elites and less powerful groups (p. 240). Although Gramsci described intellectuals as the dominant group's "deputies" (1999, p. 141)—because they work on behalf of those whose interest it is to maintain hegemony and keep dominant ideologies in place—intellectuals also hold the potential power to *resist* hegemony, bringing along those whom they influence (Zompetti, 1997).

"Gramsci's wide-ranging concern with intellectuals and education suggests a close and careful scrutiny of the role of media" as an important knowledge source, Landy (1994) observed (p. 10). Because media content serves as a form of literature—a cultural production—the connection between Gramsci and the importance of understanding how ideology becomes inculcated into the wider culture thus that he paid close attention to media as a way to convey knowledge (by those with access to those communication channels) and as a way to challenge that knowledge. Indeed, as Dombroski (1986) articulated, Gramsci's writings "are all based on the premise that literature represents definite social realities" which can manipulate or educate people, based on their social conditioning (p. 115). As intellectuals, the writers of literature—and, by extension films, television shows, advertisements, and all manner of media incarnations—have the power to not only "act upon human conscience," but also to transform society (p. 115). Herein we find how Gramsci's vision of a new and more democratic culture begins with the leadership that intellectuals provide, intellectuals not only in terms of thinkers and philosophers, but of writers and journalists (Holub, 1992).

Here we come back to Gramsci's declaration that everyone has the capacity to be an intellectual in the sense of having an intellect and using it (Gramsci, 1999). Gramsci celebrated the agency of the individual and the ability of people to think for themselves: "Gramsci argued that human consciousness had a role to play in the historical process. What he felt was required was that people should become aware of their own historical position. Accordingly, he believed that the starting point of any revolutionary activity necessitated a concerted effort devoted to raising the awareness level of the populace" (Trepanier, 1991, p. 38). Gramsci argued that when we become aware of the fact that ideology is produced not by ourselves as individuals, but by distant elites for their own benefit, we realize that "only through a massive change in cultural awareness can the hegemony be threatened," Zompetti (1997, p. 77). In other words, until a majority of people becomes aware of their own capacity to produce alternatives to the given hegemony and asserts a creative role built on their own interests, then freedom will remain unrealized, and self-determination likely won't happen.

GRAMSCI AND MEDIA LITERACY

So, how do people become aware of the ideologies that influence them, that form a culture's shared beliefs, values, and practices, and that prevent them from realizing there are alternatives that offer the potential for a more equitable and just system? One way is through becoming literate about the meanings that imbue the movies and television shows we watch that tell us, either overtly or covertly, what the culture in which we live expects of us. Media literacy refers to "the understanding we have about the ways in which media affect ourselves, our society, and our culture" (Natharius, 2004, p. 38). Natharius, in addressing the importance of visual awareness regarding media images, particularly their content, composition, and references to previous, recognizable, and familiar images, offers an axiom that aptly applies to all forms of media awareness: "The more we know, the more we see" (p. 238). Though speaking to the importance of the visuality of images, Natharius's axiom also applies more broadly to the power we gain when we bring our own knowledge to the consumption of media. We can detect concepts, theories, ideologies, or philosophies conveyed through a media text's images, dialogue, or narratives because we already have learned about them. For example, our knowledge of Shakespeare's *Hamlet*, written between 1599 and 1601, helps us to appreciate and recognize similar characters, storylines, and themes in the FX television network series *Sons of Anarchy*, a drama about a California motorcycle gang that aired from 2008 to 2014. The more we know about Shakespearean plays, the more we see their elements when we encounter new forms of entertainment that find their basis in those plays.

Media literacy finds its foundation in the idea that, as individuals, we can come to see media as constructions built out of particular sets of conventions, designed to appeal to us as audience members, and appear simple enough to need no critique. We understand these constructions as a force of hegemony when we work toward critique. Early cultural studies theorists identified critique, and the encouragement of cultural actors—that is, everyone involved in cultural production and consumption—to become critics, as a way to understand the negotiation between dominant, resistant, and residual readings of media. With roots in the adult education movement, which championed educational opportunities for regular people and not just the elites, the study of culture meant paying as much attention to the dance hall as elite theatre and opera, to the dime novel as much as elite literature. For early cultural theorists in Birmingham and at the Open University in the United Kingdom during the 1960s, understanding power in culture meant understanding the popular arts, as opposed to the fine arts, as suggested by Stuart Hall and Paddy Whannell (1963). Cultural studies scholars were fundamentally interested in coming to understand how audience members organized their political agency through the popular culture they consumed; they went on to conduct deep investigations into the way participation with media texts shaped political meanings.

Those who have taken the Gramscian path to studying mass media content and popular culture see hegemony as a framework for analyzing this site of ideological distribution. "As an analytical construct, hegemony also highlights the media's relationship to social and political change, especially the interaction between media institutions and alternative social movements that challenge the political order," explained Carragee (1993, p. 331). Cultural studies theorists find Gramsci's theory of hegemony useful as they strive to understand how culture operates as dominant discourse, and its potential for liberation (Zompetti, 2012). Indeed, lines of inquiry inspired by Gramsci's theories and that articulate the interconnectedness of hegemony, cultural production, and mass media have addressed their composite "web of power" (Jones, 2006, p. 3), with a plethora of studies addressing a wide range of applicable topics, such as political communication, transnational media structures, news coverage and news systems, economic ownership, and popular culture entertainment.[12] In short, the mass media en masse becomes the field upon which Gramsci's "unstable equilibria" play out, where the "systematic tendency" to reproduce a structure of domination meets counteracting tendencies that push back against hegemonic ideologies (Hall, 1977, p. 346).

In short, critical media/cultural studies "theorizes the interconnections between culture and communication, and how they constitute each other" (Kellner, 2009, p. 103). Kellner further explicated the qualities that define this approach to studying media by noting it aims to foster awareness of the ways in which media illustrate the hegemonic struggle between dominance and resistance, and the ways to make people critical and informed media consumers and producers. This involves a viewpoint that addresses social bias based on class, gender, race, sexual orientation, and other ways people suffer from discrimination, and criticizes media that promote bias and oppression. The point of learning how to critically examine media artifacts is to teach people to become media literate, critical thinkers who have the power to resist being manipulated, and instead maintain values that support their own interests, rather than the interests of empowered others.

This is why we find Gramsci not only relevant to the understanding of mass media today but especially important in arguing for a media literate audience. Gramsci's theories offer critical insights into how mass media industries serve as conduits for ideologies. Gramsci's development of arguments around hegemony has even more relevance in the twenty-first century than when he first wrote them. Gramsci's statement that we are all intellectuals, even if we don't all function as intellectuals in a professional sense, is more important and cogent than ever, even though Gramsci's writing took place in an earlier technological and historical era, wrote Landy (1994). This continues to serve as our belief as teachers and advocates of media literacy. We rely on Gramsci's prescient and prognostic thinking for deconstructing ideologies detected in mass media, and for considering those resistant positions that play the role of opposing forces that illustrate the cyclical process of hegemony.

To approach an inquiry armed with Gramsci's ideas, Bové (1994) cautioned,

> does not mean that we should simply apply Gramscian notions in the analysis of contemporary realities or that we should entertain certain notions simply because they carry the imprimatur of Gramsci. Rather, we should think *like* Gramsci, work *as* he did in trying to understand his own political defeat and that of his movement. (p. ix)

If we can successfully apply Gramsci's analytic practices to our contemporary media environment, we still might fail to ascend to a full socialist state, but understanding our own media experiences has enormous transformative potential, from seeing the way media re-inscribe caustic ideas about identity tied to race, gender, class, and sexual orientation, to working to extend the possibilities of alternative hegemonies that build off of complex intersectional identities and experiences. Although everyone holds the potential for becoming an intellectual—that is, to think critically in one's own right, not as in a professional sense, and then acquiring the skills to express one's ideas—the problem of becoming a culture producer is one of access to the communicative platforms that can influence the wider society. In a Gramscian worldview, cultural production equates to cultural power. The question then becomes: How can alternatives to hegemonic messages, and, hence, hegemonic thinking, find their way to the audiences that need them the most?

CHAPTER PREVIEWS

In many ways, one can view Gramsci as a parent of media literacy and its efforts to find a place in formal education. Many educators have worked for decades to position media literacy as a set of questions, practices, and skills that enable any student at any age to develop and deploy their own intellectual potential in the face of their media experiences. In discussing the significance of Gramsci to media, turning to education is critical. In chapter 2, we discuss the relationship between Gramscian ideas of education and of media. Hegemony plays a central and complicated role in relation to the development of a cultural "common sense," especially in the effort to advance media literacy and transform it into critical media literacy. As technological change, economic imperatives, and regulatory patterns have transformed our media environment, applying Gramsci's ideas to the tension between legacy and digital media parallels hegemonic tensions illustrated by the difference between learning and "common sense."

The mass media play the role of cultural producers in a Gramscian approach to media literacy, and Hollywood serves as the major cultural production center. Chapter 3, "Gramsci, Film, TV, and Cable Streaming: Toward Counterhegemony," focuses on how hegemony plays out onscreen. In that culture and inequality of class served as the central theme of Gramsci's writings, noted Crehan (2016), examining culture through Hollywood's portrayals of the human experience helps us as critical viewers to uncover the lived inequalities in daily life. Inequality marks facets of everyday existence, and its portrayal appears in cultural products proffered by the entertainment industry. In Hollywood's production of culture, we can see a tension between the forging of a media-produced "folklore" and storytelling practices that offer scripts telling us how to live, whether in terms of the construction of "race" and the move toward antiracism, or gender and the effects of the #MeToo movement. In chapter 3, this is explored through examinations of television shows and films that illustrate these aspects of hegemony.

In chapters 4 and 5, we look at how popular entertainment media serve as sites of hegemonic struggle regarding gender. In that gender equality and inequality relate to differences not only between genders but within genders, hegemonic thinking reinforces ideas about the appropriate behaviors associated with an individual's sex. Whereas much research in this area of media study has focused on the portrayal of women, in particular, we approach gender hegemony here using the lens of masculinity as a way to examine the privileging not only of one gender over another but one way of thinking about what it means to "be a man" over others. Regarding the performance of masculinity and the inequalities between culturally dictated versions of masculinity, media portrayals that rely on commonsense notions about manhood thus reveal the power of hegemony in civil society. Chapter 4, "Hegemonic Masculinity in the Mass Media," serves as a review of the concept of hegemonic masculinity, the culturally dominant form of masculinity in a given setting. This concept, which originated in women's studies, explains why mass media tend to replicate a certain version of masculinity, which in turn supports ongoing gender inequality in which women are viewed as secondary to men within a patriarchy.

Chapter 5, "The Gendered *Endgame*: Marvel's New Man," presents a case study of hegemonic masculinity, which legitimates unequal gender relations through the reinforcement of particular sets of accepted and prevailing behaviors associated with cultural ideals of manhood. We examine the 2019 international hit film *Avengers: Endgame*, the action-fantasy denouement of Marvel Entertainment's Avengers cinematic franchise, and how it illustrates hegemonic struggle by affirming or modifying elements of versions of mediated masculinity that uphold particular ideas of manhood. We then situate our analysis within an overall treatment of gender in the film and discuss its implications within a Gramscian context.

In our conclusion, chapter 6, we summarize the ways in which hegemony, cultural studies, and media literacy offer opportunities to develop deeper, more critical ways of experiencing the media's influences on culture. We revisit Gramsci's relevance in terms of the hegemonic struggle between traditional and newer media forms, such as online streaming. Finally, we suggest media issues for future research that seeks to understand the relationship between audiences and media producers, who essentially trade places when we think of transmedia development, audience studies and fan fiction, and the redeployment of images as memes and gifs that resonate with their varied audiences. We raise the question of how a Gramscian analysis would make sense of these developments, and how we might use his work to understand hegemonic politics in daily life.

NOTES

1. Although people have studied Gramsci's political and social theories for decades, there exists an area of Gramscian studies on Gramsci himself. For example, Forgacs (2016) explicated how Gramsci's disability influenced his personal and

political identity, and how the now-classic photograph of Gramsci as a young man echoes similar images of past revolutionaries. Forgacs noted that the iconic and "instantly recognisable" photo portrait of Gramsci, which graces the covers of books on Gramsci, including *The Antonio Gramsci Reader* (2000), edited by Forgacs himself, was displayed in branches of the Italian Communist Party and Gramsci institutes, much in the way photographs of presidents and emperors have hung on the walls of governmental offices and even in people's homes (Forgacs, 2016, p. 346). The work of Swiss artist Thomas Hirshhorn, known for his politically inspired creations, produced a temporary artwork titled "Gramsci Monument" in the Bronx, New York, in 2013. It served as another example of Gramsci-related work outside the expected focus on political and social theory in published treatments. Hirschhorn wrote an article about it, explaining his motivation was "because I love the work and the life of Antonio Gramsci" (2015, p. 214). An installation consisting of a painting of Gramsci's iconic photographic portrait in the style of street art, a complex of wooden structures built with the help of area residents, and workshops and seminars, Hirschhorn's "participatory sculpture" honoring Gramsci even included a display of Gramsci's personal items (Johnson, 2013, p. C19). While an art review in *The New York Times* titled "A Summer Place in the South Bronx" included a brief explanation of Gramsci's theory of hegemony ("a worldview of society" that "keeps people in their place"), the transitory nature of the installation and the lackluster attendance at the time of the reviewer's visit resulted in the conclusion that it was just another project by Hirschhorn, rather than what the reviewer had hoped would be an inspiring experience (Johnson, 2013, p. C19).

2. Hall (1986) noted that Gramsci did not originate the term "hegemony," as it was used by Lenin in an "analytic sense to refer to the leadership which the proletariat [working class] in Russia was required to establish over the peasantry in the struggles to found a socialist state" (p. 15). Thus, hegemony serves as the result of "winning a substantial degree of popular consent" (p. 15). Harris (2015) explained that Gramsci employed the term's use in order to highlight the cultural and political aspects of class, particularly class struggle in Italy. The socialist/communist revolution that Gramsci worked toward would impose the hegemony—the dominance—of the working class.

3. This dominance plays a key role in the concept of hegemony, with the caveat that social power and political leadership in the form of civil institutions comes with consent, not direct force (Artz and Murphy, 2000; Bates, 2002; Femia, 2002: Jones, 2006; Martin, 2002; Sassoon, 1982). Aside from how ruling groups implicitly hold power, hegemony also connects to how one political player enjoys a dominant role in international relations, and how that role can be contested. For example, Collins et al. (2004) examined how the United States' role as hegemon/world leader was contested by the European press.

4. For more on definitions of "culture," see Jandt (2013).

5. See also Landy (2008). Dominant ideologies also are conveyed by sporting events and accompanying rituals using national symbols of unity that assist in disguising differences between region and class, as noted by Harris (2015).

6. Gramsci wrote "man," but as an example of his own views on the hegemony of language use and to avoid gendered language in which masculine pronouns were used as part of common sense, we use "person" here.

7. Steiner's explanation of hegemony's points of weakness as a social force stemmed from a personal conversation with one of the authors related to the hegemony of weddings and their depiction in wedding and bridal media in 2007.

8. The lists of Gramsci-relevant disciplines provided by Filippini (2017) and Thomas (2009) are not exhaustive; Racine (2009) applied Gramsci's writings on hegemony to nursing education and the importance of culturally safe nursing practices on a global scale. Briziarelli and Guillem's (2016) study of social mobilization (naturally) found application of Gramsci to their analysis of social movements in Italy, Spain, and the Occupy Wall Street movement in the United States.

9. Landy (2008) explained that Gramsci paid little attention to radio and cinema as particular modes of cultural production because of his imprisonment; he was removed from society and therefore did not have access to them. The nature of radio at that time in Italy was controlled by the Fascist regime; by the mid-1930s radio was not only used to broadcast propaganda and information, but also entertainment. Regarding cinema, Landy noted, Italian cinema was highly influential, but by the end of the 1920s had "gone into eclipse" (p. 104).

10. Regarding intellectuals as a profession, Gramsci's emphasis on inclusivity, which marked his commitment to mass movements, applied as well; Forgacs (2016) noted that Gramsci himself "had little patience with intellectuals who liked to remain within their own closed circle" (p. 354).

11. We base these descriptions on explanations by Femia (2010) and Sassoon (1982). Gramsci wrote extensively on intellectuals and their functions and categories based on situatedness, and education as a system within civil society. We discuss this further in chapter 2.

12. Numerous scholarly works address these aspects of Gramscian thought applicable to the study of mass media in some form; we cite even more studies most relevant to our analyses of media texts in subsequent chapters. Related to film studies, in *Film, Politics, and Gramsci*, Landy (1994) applied Gramscian concepts to her analyses of Italian and British cinema. Rodriguez (2018) explained how Hollywood's Motion Picture Production Code of 1930 imposed a hegemony on the content of films, with its morality rules originating from purely economic reasons. Research of the media industry invokes Gramsci by taking a "hegemony-adjacent" approach; see Carragee (1993) for a review of research on news industry content and practices that contribute to this area of media studies and Zompetti's (2012) list of research studies on popular television programs that demonstrate the utility of entertainment as a mechanism for ideological instruction. Treatments that analyze the hegemonic implications of journalistic reporting of and use of media by hegemons—the leading or major powers (particularly the United States)—include those by Boukala (2019) and Collins et al. (2004). Simon (2013) analyzed *Time* magazine's coverage of its "person of the year" female corporate whistleblowers and how they challenge hegemonic boundaries of gender as well as serve as organic intellectuals. Rowe's (2004) essay explored hegemonic processes and the imposition of dominant ideology in sports.

Chapter 2

A Gramscian Approach to Media Literacy

In many ways the contemporary state of media literacy in relation to education has finally, in the era of social media and digital reproduction and manipulation, caught up with Antonio Gramsci's ideas about the force of education outlined so many years ago. To make this argument, it will be necessary to, first, outline what we mean when we talk and think about media literacy education, especially critical media literacy education. Second, we can consider the transformations of media literacy education over time and their relationship with ideology and hegemony grounded in Gramsci's thinking. Finally, we can talk about the larger ways that a culture develops paths for contending with its media environments, some of which would follow from Gramsci's suggestions, but some of which perpetuate interests that disempower people either going through an educational process, or whose ways of thinking did not sufficiently engage in a critical practice that serves their interests, as media experiences have grown in scale and scope.

Through this examination, we see a clear underlying idea: the articulation of ideology and hegemony does not equate to a process of rote indoctrination of inert and static ideas. At whatever age—actually, at every age—people live in a dynamic, changing, moving environment of cultural forces, and they embody these forces through social practices (Fischman and McLaren, 2005, p. 426). In the contemporary environment, we must take into account the dialogic possibilities of the current media environment; to the extent that individuals wish to be producers of media, they make aesthetic, intellectual, and affective contributions to the media sphere. How they wish to be producers and consumers of media directly relates to their understanding of the role that a media context plays in their lives. Facts and opinions swirl around them, just as facts and opinions flow among the people around them, and any resulting interaction reflects the complex points view that give their participation

27

meaning. Gramsci referred to groups who are excluded or displaced from the hierarchies of power as the "subaltern." As Gramsci (1971) saw it,

> It is almost always the case that a "spontaneous" movement of the subaltern classes is accompanied by a reactionary movement of the right wing of the dominant class, for concomitant reasons. An economic crisis, for instance, engenders on the one hand discontent among the subaltern classes and sponta- neous mass movements, and on the other conspiracies among the reactionary groups, who take advantage of the objective weakening of the government in order to attempt coups d'état. (p. 199)

That combination of action and meaning plays a role in the perpetuation of ideology and the performance of hegemony. Whether they reflect cooperation with dominant power or question and critique dominant power can offer some indication of what is at stake. This may reflect the difference between a media literate person and a *critically* media literate person.

CRITICAL MEDIA LITERACY IN EDUCATION

Media literacy education centrally concerns the efforts to give individuals the tools to understand their media environment, to participate and contribute to it positively in some sense, and to deepen their understanding of their role as both an individual and a member of a culture and a society. Positively "in some sense" suggests that being a media producer and a media consumer comes with responsibilities, since the central effects have to do with the rela- tionship between individuals and collectives.

For the sake of thinking about media experience, we need to consider the artificial separation between content and form—between what a mes- sage communicates and how it communicates. In our typical experience, the content draws attention, and form usually falls away as an object of scrutiny. But meaning results through the relationship between what is said or shown, and how it is said or shown. The separation is artificial, because pure form never exists without content, any more than there can be content without form. As obvious as this might seem, an education developing the skills to put this artificial separation into intellectual practice becomes problematic for a variety of reasons, from the assumption that form serves as a mere vehicle for the transmission of a message to the idea that forms are neutral in regard to the meaning of the content. Message creators often select a form so it will not get in the way of the message. Thus, they somewhat intentionally divert attention from the form of communication, as if they see form as a distraction or a kind of "noise."

Media literacy education often faces suspicions that one is being manipulated below the level of conscious understanding. At an extreme this can turn into a conspiracy theory about media manipulation (consider the use of subliminal messaging, or backward masking, or hiding images airbrushed within advertisements). Media literacy education frequently addresses these issues, and many instances of manipulation exist, but it happens more significantly at the surface level, as a characteristic of how communication happens at all.

Perhaps the best way to understand media literacy education is to see it as a series of questions that are asked of a media experience. This often requires a conscious effort on the part of the individual working toward critical literacy to interrupt the flow of the media experience in order to examine it more closely. This might mean a pause in the linear process of a flowing narrative, such as pausing a movie or a commercial to think and talk about it. It also might mean just a shift in attention, so that, say, a person views a still image of an advertisement with a focused interrogation. The implication of this approach underscores the overall point of media literacy education: to disrupt the control over the mediated moment and shift it to the observer.

Interrogating a message typically involves the individual (alone, in a group, or in a classroom) asking a series of questions about the media experience. For example, NAMLE, the National Association for Media Literacy Education (formerly the American Media Literacy Association), offers a list of ten such questions in its "Key Questions When Analyzing Media Messages":

1. Authorship: Who made this message?
2. Purpose: Why was this made? Who is the target audience (and how do you know)?
3. Economics: Who paid for this?
4. Impact: Who might benefit from this message? Who might be harmed by it? Why might this message matter to me?
5. Response: What kinds of actions might I take in response to this message?
6. Content: What is this about (and what makes you think that)? What ideas, values, information, and/or points of view are overt? Implied? What is left out of this message that might be important to know?
7. Techniques: What techniques are used? Why were those techniques used? How do they communicate the message?
8. Interpretations: How might different people understand this message differently? What is my interpretation of this and what do I learn about myself from my reaction or interpretation?
9. Context: When was this made? Where or how was it shared with the public?

10. Credibility: Is this fact, opinion, or something else? How credible is this
    (and what makes you think that)? What are the sources of the informa-
    tion, ideas, or assertions?[1]

Asking these questions and having to develop answers in some form (discussion, group presentation, or argument writing, for example) plays the important role of using language to describe the effects of the media experience.
Keep in mind, however, that this takes hard work, because in most cases
media creators design their messages to be taken in without any complex
interrogation. Media messages are designed to go down easy, but a media
literacy interrogation process is designed to make the going much rougher.

Critical media literacy can follow all of these same procedures, but it
specifically focuses on the relations of power that imbue these media experiences. The term "critical" holds a variety of different implications about the
intellectual process taking place. Almost all versions are built on a reflective
practice of knowing, especially understanding the differences between what
is actually seen or argued, and how individuals make sense of what is seen
or argued. If we consider sense making as a system of judgments, then a
critical approach seeks to understand the thinking process that leads to well-
supported judgments.

By focusing on the thinking process, this notion of "thinking" can suffer, as Peters (2007) pointed out, from a tendency to become acultural and
ahistorical, not focusing on contexts in time and space, but instead focusing
on supposedly universal processes of logic and reasoning. In the same way,
we might detect that elements of a media production (under, for example,
the question "What techniques are used?") connect to a particular meaning
in the moment, but we may find different nuances when we also consider the
context of a particular media experience. Burbules and Berk (1999) noted that
this sense of "critical" perhaps may mean "self-aware," but it is less invested
in understanding the *conditions* of meaning, which are typically reflected in
the historical and cultural context that must be taken into account. Critical
thinking in this sense thus focuses "on the more inclusive problem of people
basing their life choices on unsubstantiated truth claims—a problem that is
nonpartisan in its nature and effects" (p. 46). Like recent attention being paid
to "fake news" and the proliferation of false information, these are significant
ways of thinking that are fundamental to determining the truth value of a
thought or image.

Critical media literacy, alternately, goes beyond interest in the reliability
question by using critical inquiry to explore the surrounding contexts of
culture and history to examine how power is manipulated in these media
experiences. Critical media literacy strives to understand who benefits from
a particular interpretation, and how power is distributed, both unequally and

among hierarchies. Critical media literacy has two ultimate goals: to produce individuals who are (1) self-sufficient in their understanding of their media experiences and (2) liberated by their critical understanding of media.

In addition to the ten key questions for analyzing media, a critical media literacy approach attempts to address how culture becomes reproduced in educational contexts. Specific ideas about race and antiracism, for example, might come from the careful examination of representations in films and television, memes and symbols in social media, as well as a knowledge of history that reflects carefully on who organizes the historical story being told, and how that storytelling process reflects choices made by the storyteller rather than accepting the details on their face and not examining the ways of telling. Representations of race, gender, and sexualities present areas that require particular sensitive examination, especially since power relations and social hierarchies become established in these webs of meaning.

Looking at sexism, racism, class conflict, and other aspects of society in this part of the critical examination focuses on the question: Who benefits? The fourth question from NAMLE's list addresses the impact of a media message. Asking this question leads to its inverse: Who is disadvantaged or oppressed? Thus, a critical media literacy approach works toward the realization of social justice, and at the same time connects the interests of the individual thinker to the larger community. This becomes a critical component when considering how a Gramscian approach illuminates the teaching and learning of media literacy.

THE GRAMSCIAN INFLUENCE

In his discussion of Gramsci and hegemony in *Marxism and Literature*, Williams (1977) emphasized the "wholeness" of the process of hegemony. Williams saw in Gramsci a discrimination between "rule" (or domination) and hegemony:

> "Rule" is expressed in directly political forms and in times of crisis by direct or effective coercion. But the more normal situation is a complex interlocking of political, social, and cultural forces, and "hegemony," according to different interpretations, is either this or the active social and cultural forces which are its necessary elements. (p. 108)

As with much of the work that makes up media literacy, we can examine the articulation between elements that coerce versus elements that use more subtle means to manipulate desires and actions. As Williams argued, hegemony includes both the notion of culture as the whole way of life that individuals convince themselves are a product of their own efforts and ideological components that represent the interest of a particular class in its efforts to maintain power and capital. Ideology presents as more formal, more systemic, more fixed in our experience. Hegemony as a way of living in a culture where ideological ideas dominate turns it into something experienced as common sense, or a thought considered so obvious that it requires no special re-examination.

The source of this common sense brings to attention one of the central controversies that swirled in Gramsci's thinking. This involves the differentiation between the state and what he referred to as "civil society." As Holub (1992) argued, Gramsci's ideas about hegemony required a more complex notion of social structure than a binary polarization of the individual and the state. Power in Gramsci's view is not just imposed on the individual but distributed through social and cultural institutions like religious organizations, educational institutions, and the media (especially journalism). These institutions, through their power, then reconstitute a negotiated version of dominant ideologies traveling through these civil agents into ideas of family structure, identity, and the terms of civil and social participation. The critical sites of the negotiation of power shift through historical eras; while that negotiation was made in the context of working-class life in the modern era, it shifts to service sector work in the postmodern era, explained Holub. In the twenty-first century, the negotiation of civil society happens as we manage our physical selves in relation to our digital selves, where social media grows into yet another set of significant cultural institutions.

In addition to the shift from working-class life to service sector work, hegemonic power is exerted by transnational organizations, usually under private control operating under capitalist mandates. As they cross national boundaries, they are subject to some amount of regulatory influence, reflecting the power dynamics of complex networked organizations. Under these conditions, regulations imposed in one place may instigate a change in all the places that the social media site is used. Efforts in the European Union, for example, to make sure EU internet users are aware of the use of tracking routines has meant that users in countries with less regulation, like the United States, are presented with the same notification system (and agreement buttons that need to be clicked). Although these efforts are motivated by the desire to put more power into the hands of users, whether that empowerment is real or illusory remains a question of hegemony.

Critical media literacy, then, involves the desire for a deeper understanding of how these cultural institutions bridge from legacy (pre-digital) media to the complex social organizations found on the network of multiple social media "locations" such as Facebook, Instagram, TikTok, YouTube, Twitter, and the many other places where the cultural adaptation from legacy to digital takes place. Even when these transnational networked media systems contain greater amounts of user-generated content, their potential to "democratize" media are re-negotiated via state and corporate power to severely limit the control individuals have over media systems. In fact, the crisis of a shared understanding of a fact-based worldview is challenged by state and corporate persuasion that seeks to maintain regimes of power even when their claims fail to be factually sustainable. As Gramsci might observe, this can displace a subaltern understanding of the historical conditions of civil society. It also can create an illusion of empowerment, without ever really shifting control over the media away from state, corporate, and commercial private interests that dominate control over networked social media.

Another effect of this merger of civil society with social media involves the struggle between scientific consensus and hegemonic power. These frequently come into conflict when, for example, the mounting evidence of long-term destruction of the environment through global warming threatens the power of corporate activity. Through corporate public relations' participation in the contemporary digital civil sphere, culture becomes part of a discursive battle over the concept of science (Jacques et al., 2019). As Gramsci's exploration of hegemony argued, this then turns into a conflict between the rules of scientific evidence and common sense. "Critical" skepticism becomes a tool used to undermine faith in scientific consensus, as questioning the power and motivations of the scientific community then leads to an accusation that scientists work on behalf of special and private interests. Those who accept this as part of their "common sense" response to issues of environmental sustainability neglect to question the agents of power that advocate for this (non-)critical position.

This misapplication of a "critical" perspective enjoys success as long as the individuals involved do not reflect on the powerful sources injecting an anti-science perspective into civil society. But looking at the motivations of those sources of persuasion—and reflexively considering the terms of power that they deploy—is not encouraged when faced with the combination of common sense and confirmation bias. Reflexive examination, which critical media literacy fundamentally asserts, seems foolish, or childishly resistant. Frequently in attempting a critical media analysis this generates a response similar to something like "You are reading too much into it" (see Beliveau, 2011). At the same time, those who oppose "reading too much into it" see critical media literacy as destructive of the pleasure of media, reinforcing an antagonism between experiencing media as pleasure and the difficulty of critical evaluation. In the same way, school becomes viewed as a taxing and frequently boring set of institutional experiences, providing a mix of functional literacy skills, intangible STEM (science, technology, engineering, and math) sequences, and the difficult process of analyzing what one reads. Though cliché, these views posit a tension between the pleasurable consumption of media as easy, obvious, and fun, and the critical consideration of media as unpleasant, hard, and obscure.

Hegemony, a powerful mediator between these forces, suggests that people consent and cooperate with a set of understandings that are "common sense," and therefore their own, since "common sense" does not appear to belong to anybody. Note how this hegemonic process holds the potential for critical reconsideration by, again, resisting the idea that hegemony consists of ideas that do not favor any single group. Critical reconsideration of asking who benefits from a media message can connect these ideas to a particular group who gains something from their popular acceptance. Here again we find in Gramsci's writings the impetus for asking such questions:

> Thus it is incongruous that the concrete posing of the problem of hegemony should be interpreted as a fact subordinating the group seeking hegemony. Undoubtedly the fact of hegemony presupposes that account be taken of the interests and the tendencies of the groups over which hegemony is to be exercised, and that a certain compromise equilibrium should be formed—in other words, that the leading group should make sacrifices of an economic-corporate kind. But there is also no doubt that such sacrifices and such a compromise cannot touch the essential; for though hegemony is ethical-political, it must also be economic, must necessarily be based on the decisive function exercised by the leading group in the decisive nucleus of economic activity. (Gramsci, 1971, p. 161)

Hegemony allows us to understand the intersection of the pleasure connected to consuming stories, the deep desires people have for consuming media as a way of giving life meaning, and the (slightly tarnished) economic relations that lubricate the process.

The dominant class position that gains power from the distribution of the ideology over the reigning sense of reality sells it through pleasure, aligned with the economics and technologies of cultural connection. As Gramsci (1971) noted, for an ideology to gain the consent in hegemony, it must balance force and consent:

> The normal exercise of hegemony on the now classical terrain of the parliamentary regime is characterized by the combination of force and consent, which balance each other reciprocally, without force predominating excessively over consent. Indeed, the attempt is always made to ensure that force will appear to be based on the consent of the majority, expressed by the so-called organs of public opinion. (p. 80, n49)

The acceptance of this is manifest in what the individual sees as an acceptable exchange of sacrificing power for gaining access, of giving over control, or agreeing to a set of terms, perhaps. You might engage with, say, live social media that attracts you because of the context and connections it offers; if you get on the social media site, then you are not missing out. The sacrifice in power—the price—may include expensive technologies, compromised privacy, and losing the commodity value of your own information and desires. That value is vacuumed up, repackaged, and sold to other parties who then leverage (sell) that value for their benefit as a producer and at your expense as a consumer.

What Gramsci referred to as the formation of a compromise(d) equilibrium exists in the consent expressed when someone signs on, downloads an app, and interacts with it, perhaps being advertised to at the same time. Cleverly targeted ad technologies do not clearly demonstrate how they collected information about you, or how they are using information about you, but you may not mind or care at all if the result is exposure to things (commodities) that you didn't even know you wanted. You consent to the experience, you click on the ad or the "clickbait," and you experience the pleasure of the commodity.

Critical media literacy poises itself to ruin your "fun" in such a situation. It wants to make you aware of the hegemonic process, of the consent that we collectively agree to when we hit the "I agree" button and don't know what we agreed to. It wants you to experience the familiar pleasures of storytelling that reproduce racism, sexism, homophobia, attitudes toward violence, and the pleasures of crazy rich fantasy. Moreover, it wants social media participants to understand clearly the cost of participation, the information commodities that are being exchanged, and the desire on the part of the media creators for that interaction to go on with little notice and even less concern.

Critical media literacy proposes a way to critique media not just in terms of criticism, but by using a holistic approach. As an educational process, critical media literacy allows us to see how media serve as a component of economic relations, and, using the term developed by Althusser (1971), as an ideological apparatus. Our participation as media consumers becomes part of the consent required by hegemony, as we accept the bargain that social (and legacy) media offers. But critical media literacy strives to keep us aware that our own control and power are the price we pay for the pleasures and advantages of the media experiences we seek.

TRANSFORMATIONS OF MEDIA LITERACY

Media literacy (particularly in the United States) has developed outside of schools and educational institutions, because most of its history has not been included as a central part of school curriculum. But as the power of media has increased over time, the importance of understanding the intertwined nature of both consumption of media and its place in the classroom has supported the case that media literacy advocates have made to increase the dedication of time and attention to media literacy teaching within education.

One element of that transformation has to do with the late-twentieth-century understanding of media education. And it is especially important to understand the cultural boundaries that are crossed in this discussion. Raymond Williams, cited earlier, was one of several people involved in adult education in the United Kingdom during the post–World War II period championing the idea that a liberal education should be crafted for the general population, rather than just being the province of an elite.

This points to one of the difficulties involved in bringing critical attention to media. It had not been previously acknowledged that the systems of media representations were growing in significance. They were typically seen as entertainment and not worthy of serious study. In the British context this media representation served as a site for class struggle. As Steele (1997) explained, a debate that started in the 1930s and continued for several decades produced two lines of thinking about the origins of the discipline of English. In one, English was a discipline that was seen as "key to a fully humanized society in which individual creative potential could be allowed to flower in line with a maturing democracy" (p. 50). In the other, English was the

> product of the struggle of the industrial middle class for hegemony over the emerging political strength of the working class. Through the development of English studies a powerfully ideological veil could be thrown over the real needs and experiences of the working class, who would come to identify their interests with those of their political masters. (p. 50)

This debate framed English as a discipline that saw the study of literature as the route for understanding culture. Along with English, history, anthropology, and philosophy became the disciplinary routes through which the study of cultures across the lines of class would eventually develop into cultural studies.

The instructors working in adult education, some teaching in "extension" programs in British cities aimed at working-class adult students, brought to their teaching an investment in the values of working-class life and culture, including politics. Raymond Williams promoted the value of studying culture through the holistic examination of (working class) life in books like *The Long Revolution* (1961). This reflected the experiences of his own working-class background. E. P. Thompson was a historian who made his way into adult education teaching history and literature. His most influential work, *The Making of the English Working Class* (1963), depicted the growing awareness among members of the working class of their own interests, and the way their efforts reflect the struggle to maintain those interests rather than a history that contextualizes working-class educational advances in terms of the expansion of Enlightenment ideas.

Two other significant contributors to this developing focus on culture worked to create ways of tying media experience to their related work. Richard Hoggart, an adult education instructor at the University of Hull, wrote *The Uses of Literacy* in 1957, a book that pays particular attention to media as a mass culture phenomenon that has a damaging effect on organic local cultures, especially working-class cultures like the one in which Hoggart had grown up (Taylor, 2017). Hoggart (1957) argued that "mass" media benefit from an approach that permeates larger swaths of culture through massification:

> My argument is not that there was, in England one generation ago, an urban culture still very much "of the people" and that now there is only a mass urban culture. It is rather that the appeals made by the mass publicists are for a great number of reasons made more insistently, effectively and in a more comprehensive and centralised form today than they were earlier; that we are moving towards the creation of a mass culture; that the remnants of what was at least in parts an urban culture "of the people" are being destroyed; and that the new mass culture is in some important ways less healthy than the often crude culture it is replacing. (pp. 23–24)

Hoggart focused this critique on the effects of centralized media. He asserted that the broad cultural permeation of media has the effect of creating a sense of culture that pushes out any locally centered culture.[2] Hoggart offered not so much a critique of media in general but explained how the appeal of "mass" media draws people in. Media literacy offers the possibility of observing and analyzing this cultural effect, enabling individuals to have a more specific grasp on what is lost and found.

The other significant contributor to this direction was Stuart Hall. Hall's background in a middle-class Black family from Jamaica led to a British classical-style education at the College of Jamaica before he won a Rhodes Scholarship to Oxford. As his politics came to dominate his interest in Henry James, he moved into adult education in 1958, and by 1960 became the founding editor of the *New Left Review*, working with Raymond Williams and E. P. Thompson. His book *The Popular Arts*, co-authored with Paddy Whannell and published in 1963, was among the very first to take media culture—especially film—seriously as an influence on political life and values.

Along with Hoggart, Hall was central to the development of the Birmingham University Centre for Contemporary Cultural Studies (BCCCS).

Hall directed the Centre from 1969 until 1980. As Hall described it, mass communication research, defined by U.S. social scientific practices and paradigms, initially dominated the Media Group in BCCCS. But the Media Group quickly moved away from this dominance, and moved to a position of challenging some of the intellectual influences on the study of mass media. It moved away from the notion of a "direct media influence" model, replacing its behaviorist assumptions with notions of cultural ideological forces.

Chiefly through Stuart Hall's reading of Gramsci, cultural studies focused on the idea of how subaltern groups use media in modes of negotiation and resistance. Rather than simply diagnosing the power strategies of media producers, this work sought to understand what meanings were made of the texts and experiences of the receivers, emphasizing a deep understanding of culture with a combination of Western Marxist analysis and dialectically aware anthropological methods.

GRAMSCI'S NOTION OF INTELLECTUALS

Gramsci wrote about education, intellectuals, and the role of civil society during his time in prison from 1926 until his death in 1937. His influence on education would still take several decades to formulate. This eventually happened through changes in media education in the United Kingdom, which then filtered into both media and education in the United States through the 1960s and 1970s.

The relationship between teachers and intellectuals becomes important here, especially in a U.S. context, since the term "intellectual" plays a crucial role in understanding the force of Gramsci's efforts. To Gramsci, intellectual activity begins in one's internal considerations of philosophy, the spontaneous and potentially universal way of understanding the world. Language, he explained, contains a specific conception of the world, on top of which a person adds a second level of awareness and criticism. In addition to language, Gramsci (1971) described intellectuals as sorting through a dualism of "common sense" and "good sense," and then the set of beliefs, superstitions, and opinions that informed ways of seeing things and of acting.

The purposes of education directly relate to these concerns. Technical and scientific knowledge combines with a developing, long-term investment in language. Reading of fiction, nonfiction, and other forms of mass media messages is practiced along with the skills of verbal and written expression. These complete the cycle of educational experience. Teachers are intellectuals in how they implicitly follow a philosophy tied to their teaching. As Giroux (1997) argued,

[B]uilding upon my earlier studies of teachers as intellectuals in an attempt to reclaim a critical relationship between pedagogy and politics on the one hand, and democracy and schooling on the other . . . central to intellectual life is the pedagogical and political imperative that academics engage in rigorous social criticism while becoming a stubborn force for challenging false prophets, deconstructing social relations that promote material and symbolic violence, and speaking the "truth" to dominant forms of power and authority. (p. 268)

For Gramsci, the position of teachers and intellectuals, and where they overlap, has to do with a difference he defined between traditional intellectuals and organic intellectuals. Traditional intellectuals, historically connected to aloof institutions that transformed from monasteries into universities, worked to develop and achieve the goals of the classes that sought to expand their ruling ideologies. Organic intellectuals, on the other hand, arise from the class that is ruled. The hegemonic process involves a negotiation that constructs the terms under which organic intellectuals cooperate with the ruling ideology (to a certain negotiated extent). The teaching done by these organic intellectuals happens both through formal educational institutions, and outside of them in writing, in public speaking, and in making media. As Gramsci argued, they are driven by their passion to resist the received version of reality, the one in which their power over deciding their own interests has been negotiated away, and instead offer counterhegemonic perspectives that struggle for power.

THE GRAMSCIAN CULTURAL TURN

Cultural formations negotiate a hegemonic relationship with ruling ideologies. A good measure of that negotiation happens as people in a culture learn to develop critical approaches to their media environments. The movements in cultural studies worked to advance critical approaches to popular culture media, and brought significant attention to issues of identity.

The turn toward popular culture within cultural studies brought together theorists who were heavily influenced by Gramsci's thinking. The range of these influences found in the development of this thinking reached across disciplinary traditions; it drew on advances in anthropology that questioned the power relationships between researchers and the "subjects" of their research. Questions of power tied to authorship arose from the notion of how the process of representation—of deciding what to pay attention to, what to document, and who was worthy of attention—might have negative effects on individuals or groups.

The relevance of sociological work, especially Pierre Bourdieu's ideas of "doxa" and symbolic violence as collateral effects, also informed questions that cultural studies sought to answer. Bourdieu (2013) used the term "doxa" to describe how the natural and social world appears as self-evident, taken for granted, outside the realm of argument or discussion (p. 164). Though Bourdieu used the idea of doxa in various ways, many of his writings, as Deer (2012) argued,

> are all anthropological studies that seek to unveil the doxic conflation between objective social structures and subjective mental dispositions in various social fields of modern France (education, aesthetics). The aim is to make explicit the forms of misrecognized symbolic power (i.e., doxa) that underpin the implicit logic of practice, expectations and relations of those operating in these fields. Thus, the "distinction" doxa of the dominant social groups is matched by the proletarian doxa of the working classes in that both imply forms of cognition with practical implications that do not recognize the conditions of their own production. (p. 122)

This notion of the recognition and investigation of doxa closely parallels media literacy work. As Bourdieu (2013) put it, "[T]he subjective necessity and self-evidence of the commonsense world are validated by the objective consensus on the sense of the world, what is essential *goes without saying because it comes without saying*: the tradition is silent" (p. 167). Media experiences are often taken in the same way, as given, often described as being mere entertainment and distraction. Media literacy articulates that silence adds argument, description, and critique to what *goes without saying*. Critical practices in sociology and anthropology aspire to move the same way into critical self-reflection, accounting for the circumstances of their own production.

Symbolic violence, as a corresponding concept, is a property of language, image-based texts, or the other symbolic systems where meanings are imposed from without the cultural location, rather than from within. Parallel terms are *emic*, describing viewpoints from within a cultural location, and *etic*, viewpoints from outside of a cultural location, from the perspective of an observer. When the *etic* (from outside observation) differs from the *emic* (from inside), but for a number of reasons the *etic* is given priority, this presents an occasion of symbolic violence, which parallels the Gramscian notion of hegemony:

> Symbolic violence is the coercion which is set up only through the consent that the dominated cannot fail to give to the dominator (and therefore to the domination) when their understanding of the situation and relation can only use instruments of knowledge that they have in common with the dominator, which, being merely the incorporated form of the structure of the relation of

domination, make this relation appear as natural; or, in other words, when the schemes they implement in order to perceive and evaluate themselves or to perceive and evaluate the dominators (high/low, male/female, white/black, etc.) are the product of the incorporation of the (thus naturalized) classifications of which their social being is the product. (Bourdieu, 2000, p. 170)

Thus, symbolic violence occurs when your identity is decided by another, whether that happens in a research situation, or in the systems of representation that make up popular culture. Reflexive critical literacies offer the potential to address these omissions and mutilations through an analysis that focuses on power and authority.

Note how these acts of criticism focus on the relationship between ideology and hegemony. Cultural studies works toward an acknowledgment of the way meaning becomes constructed from a variety of subject positions. We must question the power of the author (that is, the power of authority) by acknowledging the possibility of alternative vantage points, such as those of gender, race, class, or disability. We, as critical consumers of media, need to unlearn the idea of a singular interpretation, that there exists only one way to articulate—and interpret—meaning.

Questioning the dominant or hegemonic code (as Stuart Hall [2019] used the term) of a media message is often seen as a threat because of the instability that this causes, but it is not a binary choice between a monolithic meaning and radical relativity. Variations and degrees of meaning can be constructed and may have the advantage of both articulating doxa (in Bourdieu's sense) and questioning the hegemony (in Gramsci's and Hall's sense). The range of meanings in culture makes sense through reflecting and addressing the conditions of power. Many of those conditions of power are set by the structure and priorities of the existing hegemony as it manifests in the educational system, and the way it makes choices to train students to gain and apply knowledge.

Gramsci's take on such issues was certainly a product of the conditions in Italy at the time he was writing about education. Gramsci thought that educational institutions needed to teach the kind of dominant language forms that students at all levels of culture would need in order to participate in the conversation about power. Gramsci's writing reflected ongoing regional power imbalances that were often manifested in language differences. Despite the unification of Italy, which was completed in 1871, there were still tangible splits in power between the north and south, as well as between regions.

Gramsci argued that the possibilities for creating a more equitable power distribution and giving the working classes the power he saw was withheld from them depended on their ability to master the dominant language forms linked to power. As Mayo (2014) argued, Gramsci's emphasis on educational rigor "and the inculcation of self-discipline, as well as the acquisition of powerful knowledge, which includes established knowledge such as the standard language, will hopefully ensure that those engaged in these projects will keep their feet firmly on the ground in their attempt to effectively bridge the cultural power divide" (p. 394). That also meant that a critical perspective would necessarily question the ideologically located dynamics of power in language and interpretation.

A Gramscian critical perspective fully recognizes the role that educational institutions play in the reproduction of the hegemony at the level of civil society. A good education came not from teachers who simply dished out facts; Gramsci described them as only "mediocre" (1971, p. 36). Teachers needed to offer the kinds of access to language and thinking that were connected to power in culture, and in the best situations would address the conditions of ideology that led to language in those forms. Teachers could accomplish this by adopting a "philosophy of praxis," as Gramsci (1971) argued:

> A philosophy of praxis cannot but present itself at the outset in a polemical and critical guise, as superseding the existing mode of thinking and existing concrete thought (the existing cultural world). First of all, therefore, it must be a criticism of "common sense," basing itself initially, however, on common sense in order to demonstrate that "everyone" is a philosopher and that it is not a question of introducing from scratch a scientific form of thought into everyone's individual life, but of renovating and making "critical" an already existing activity." (pp. 330–331)

Schools and educational institutions may play a role in ideological reproduction, but they also hold out the hope for students to learn ideological critique. The same holds true for another significant institution in Gramsci's writings: journalism.

JOURNALISM, NEWS, AND DOCUMENTARY: GRAMSCI, INFORMATION, AND PROPAGANDA

In his mid- to late twenties, Gramsci worked as a journalist at several newspapers starting in 1915 (*Il Grido del Popolo, Avanti!*, and *La Cittá Futura*). He then took over editorship of the journal *L'Ordine Nuovo* from 1919 to 1920. His involvement in worker politics and journalism continued, both of which he would have considered part of "education" in a general sense (Mayo 2017, p. 40). Gramsci's notions of journalism differ somewhat from the contemporary understanding of news production. The contemporary practice sees freedom in journalism as the ability to maintain neutrality, suggesting that objectivity serves as a fundamental goal. Gramsci thought of journalistic freedom as the ability to freely express one's deepest convictions without fear of a boss:

> I was never a professional journalist who sells his pen to those offering more money, thereby being compelled to lie constantly as part of the trade. I was the freest of journalists, always of a single opinion and I have never had to hide my deep convictions just to please some boss or ruffian. (Gramsci, cited in Santucci, 2010, p. 44)

This approach sheds light on one of the complications of the news industry as it is understood, and perhaps misunderstood. In a media sphere dominated by privately owned media (including publicly traded companies), directives underneath the professional activities have to do with the priorities of the corporate ownership.

The work of Edward S. Herman and Noam Chomsky thoroughly explores this aspect of media production. In *Manufacturing Consent: The Political Economy of Mass Media* (1988), Herman and Chomsky developed a "propaganda model" that starts with understanding corporate-produced news as primarily interested in the sale of news as a commodity to an audience and the sale of that audience to advertisers. This creates a conflict of interest between the news provider and the information needs of the public. Readers and viewers are thus offered a version of news produced through a series of corporate filters, which focus on corporate ownership, profit-making, the selection and use of sources, and "flak" machines—all elements in the political culture that produce criticism of the corporate news operations, and thus discipline them.

A final filter focuses on the source of cultural and social fear that plays a role in news construction. Herman and Chomsky, writing in 1988 toward the end of the "Cold War," which lasted between 1947 and 1991, understood this fear element as the threat of Soviet-style communism. This role has subsequently been filled by international terrorism. Taken together, Herman and Chomsky argued that these filters make up an understanding of corporate news as propaganda.

Much of this model operates within the notion of hegemony that Gramsci described. The Herman and Chomsky idea of propaganda intrinsically characterizes the way news organizations operate in conjunction with each other:

> If the other major media like the story, they will follow it up with their own versions, and the matter quickly becomes newsworthy by familiarity. If the articles are written in an assured and convincing style, are subject to no criticisms or alternative interpretations in the mass media, and command support by authority figures, the propaganda themes quickly become established as true even without real evidence. This tends to close out dissenting views even

more comprehensively, as they would now conflict with an already established popular belief. This in turn opens up further opportunities for still more inflated claims, as these can be made without fear of serious repercussions. (Herman and Chomsky, 1988, p. 34)

Although Gramsci's understanding of journalism predated a corporate news era, his skepticism of journalistic freedom due to the interference of business owners and bosses anticipated this development that came decades later. Like Chomsky and Herman, Gramsci worried about the potential for interference driven not by the need for informing the public but at the point where journalists become limited by the expectations of their business context. As propaganda, this idea of news must be offered in a way that caters to the audience's desires, thus protecting one side of the commodity exchange. In doing so, private commercial news operations play a role in supporting the hegemony of a society, in the same way that educational institutions support hegemony and protect it from external and critical ideologies.

Most importantly for Gramscian thinking, journalism plays a critical role in coming to terms with the production of a framework of the world offered to the general public, which still holds today through the development and domination of network television and radio as news sources, and, further, into the digital realm with its complexities. Journalism and education share the position of reproducers of an ideology of the world. The negotiation that takes place between individuals and the media, whether though canonical, popular, or mass cultural texts, requires an interrogation of the nature of representation (Landy, 1994, p. 4).

This is precisely where a Gramscian analysis applied to the intersection of journalism and documentary films becomes crucial. Nichols (2010) defined documentary as a film that speaks about situations and events involving real people (social actors) who present themselves to us as themselves in stories that convey a plausible proposal about, or perspective on, the lives, situations, and events portrayed. The distinct point of view of the filmmaker shapes this story into a way of seeing the historical world directly rather than as a fictional allegory. Many of the norms of mainstream journalism, even across its various forms (print, television, radio, and online), have maintained a consistent professional process that produces what audiences using "common sense" (in Gramsci's terms) understand as news. In the early twenty-first century, journalism was simultaneously rocked by a financial crisis brought on by unsustainable business models, and an epistemological crisis was brought on by a fissure in "common sense" that saw news as biased and "fake" if it did not align with conservative capitalist politics. Even through these crises, journalism held to a recognizable commitment to unbiased representations of significant events, told from a disinterested point of view and with a faith in the practicality of the ideal of objectivity.

Documentary, on the other hand, reached as much into journalism as it did personal factual storytelling, aesthetic variation, and critical investigation. In other words, documentary adopted a variety of modes of address, borrowing from the popular culture notions of personal filmmaking, the public fascination with crime and violence, and the representational vocabularies of science and history. But documentary typically targets a broadly conceived public audience, and, like, journalism, does not use obscure or specialist codes to tell stories and make arguments. In this sense, documentary (with rare exceptions) addresses an audience able to use their "common sense" to understand both the stories being told and the arguments being advanced. Common sense, in other words, serves as the defining mode of address in journalism and documentary. Media literacy argues for the critical interrogation of that notion of common sense.

FOLKLORE AND COMMON SENSE

The consequences of remaining within "common sense" raise a concern in Gramsci's thinking. While "common sense," which Gramsci paralleled with folklore, allows individuals and groups to understand the language used in media forms like journalism and documentary, it does not require critical activity of its audience. Gramsci desired to value the common perspectives among audiences composed of subaltern groups but argued that any ability they might have to change their circumstances—to struggle against domination—depended on mobilizing critique. As Landy (1994) argued,

> Folklore is not completely mindless nor is it completely negative. It could be said that it is the way that subaltern groups learn to rationalize and survive under conditions of hardship. Folklore is not self-conscious and critical, however, and without self-consciousness and criticism change is difficult if not impossible. Gramsci's revolutionary objective, therefore, was to raise the consciousness of subaltern groups and to provide them with a more critical and coherent conception of the world. Criticism would involve a recognition that, while the prevailing conceptions of the world appear useful, they are in fact inadequate. (p. 29)

One of the most important critical shifts comes when audience members understand that the media they consume—documentaries and long form journalism, for example—are produced within an ideological framework that is not necessarily expressed in the form itself. A long form journalism piece, like an extensive investigation or a series of pieces of a single story, may build on its association with a recognizable media brand (NBC, or *The New York Times*, or the BBC). While the brand helps to define the context that the audience uses to understand a media experience, it does not encourage a critique of the ideological motivations of that brand. It remains for the audience member to adopt a critical perspective that seeks to understand their hegemonic relationship to that brand. A documentary like *The Great Hack*, released in 2019 and credited as "A Netflix Original Documentary," does not require an individual investigation into the motivations of Netflix for being involved in the production, though online criticism and reviews may try to probe deeper into the motivations of a brand like Netflix in understanding how the film was made and distributed. This kind of criticism moves a step closer to media literacy.

Critical viewers need to make a similar adjustment to the position advocated in a media literacy framework, as discussed earlier. Most critical perspectives require asking questions about power, economics, representation, and authority. One can consume a piece of documentary media without having shifted to a critical stance, but that leaves subaltern audience members in a position in which they have no hope of understanding, much less changing, the conditions of power. Audience members using "common sense" require very little knowledge to consume the story or the argument, but for them to move to a position of "good sense" requires a reflective interaction with the media text. This means asking the kinds of questions listed earlier in this chapter to gain a full perspective on the media text. Netflix, like the BBC or 20th Century Fox, is more than just a means of distribution, as uninvolved as the brand name of the TV you are watching the documentary on. These media creators and distributors play a critical role, and good sense needs to be interested in understanding how the role influences the meaning of the media text.

CONCLUSION

Gramsci developed his ideas in the face of the advance of Italian Fascism. He built his approach to media on the fundamental significance of the material conditions and the historical circumstances of subaltern groups—the people for which he theorized the tools to interrogate power. The overlaps between a variety of media contributed to his sense of the "language" out of which people learn and come to understand their political situation. All of the elements of communication that are available to be read either reinforce the current hegemony or offer the opportunity to question and resist it.

Gramsci saw the importance of a common language in the struggle for liberation. He focused a great deal of energy on "The Southern Question," noting the way subaltern classes from his native Sardinia were treated in the northern parts of Italy. Trained as a linguist, Gramsci understood the significance of language to understanding the historical circumstances in which classes find themselves. Language, considered broadly as the communication resources used to gain information (in journalism and history) and experience drama (in the arts) in all contexts of learning, uses various media forms and contexts to construct a worldview in a cultural context.

This shift toward a common Italian language serves as the site where the hegemonic constructions of institutional education, journalism, and other media come together. Their use of language to teach or to inform can be taken in without critical reflection, and can come to construct common sense meanings of the world without interrogation. We may find ourselves educated, informed, and entertained in a system of representations that requires little regular critical reflection, and subject subaltern groups to the reigning hegemony. These media and institutions of education, information, and cultural experience (offered as entertainment but playing a much larger role in cultural construction than that) become ideological apparatuses that reproduce themselves in our identities and in our culture.

The negotiation that results in a hegemonic regime can sometimes offer the appearance of innovation, perhaps allowing for stories that reflect the experience of subaltern groups. We might see underrepresented groups (gender, race, LGBTQIA+, and class) more prominently visible, but not in a way that truly threatens the existing hegemonic order, and almost never in a way that critiques the structures and tactics of hegemony altogether. A committed critical media literacy perspective swims upstream most of the time to critique these structures, struggling against the reproduction of transnational capitalism, neoliberalism, and consumerism, which are fundamentally structured to maintain the differences between genders, races, classes, and other ways of categorizing human beings.

A Gramscian perspective offers the possibility of becoming aware of the processes of hegemony. The negotiations and compromises that outwardly defer to the individual, seen as the act of individual choices of what to consume in the media, all the while make demands that shift power away from that individual. Becoming educated, being entertained, and remaining informed seem to be processes that we as individuals manage. But under a more critical analysis it becomes clear how we are, in fact, being managed, even discouraged, from subjecting these educational and media experiences to any serious criticism. In the next chapter, we consider how critical movie viewing offers a way to examine the difference between hegemonic and counterhegemonic media.

NOTES

1. List is available at https://namle.net/wp-content/uploads/2020/10/NAMLE-Key -Qs.pdf. The National Association for Media Literacy Education (NAMLE) offers media literacy tools for all educational levels. In line with its mission, the list itself includes the statement: "Reproduction for educational purposes is encouraged."

2. Rushkoff (2010) would follow on this idea in the digital era when he described how "digital networks are decentralized technologies." "They work from far away," he continued, "exchanging intimacy for distance. This makes them terrifically suitable for long-distance communication and activities, but rather awful for engaging with what—or who—is right in front of us. By using a dislocating technology for local connection, we lost our sense of place as well as our home field advantage" (p. 35). See also Meyrowitz (1986), *No Sense of Place: The Impact of Electronic Media on Social Behavior.*

Chapter 3

Gramsci, Film, TV, and Cable Streaming

Toward Counterhegemony

Being educated, informed, and entertained intertwine with each other when we consider the terms of hegemony and the establishment of a relationship to media. In the twenty-first century, this relationship has increased in complexity as civil society tries to live between the inherited forms of media and communication that existed before the digital revolution, which we can think of as media's legacy forms, and the rapid transformations that suture their position via social media, surveillance culture, reality television, influencers, "unboxers," and varieties of social media performance. The transformations wrought by the interactions between the legacy and the digital are ongoing, so they can best be understood and discussed as snapshots in time.

Incorporating a Gramscian perspective suggests, however, that we see any snapshot as a product of historical material conditions, a process best understood when we require a critical analytic perspective to be deployed. This means seeing how power becomes manifested in the kinds of stories told through a complex conglomeration of media production under the metonymy of "Hollywood." As a source of cultural production, this term covers a vast and interconnected network, wherein ideology becomes reified and distributed throughout a borderless media world.

This chapter sketches out the expanding global notion that "Hollywood" presents to the world, especially through a Gramscian understanding of the interactions of ideology and hegemony. It postulates that the products of "Hollywood" offer a kind of intellectual activity that complicates the notion of traditional and organic intellectuals. Our discussion concludes with an attempt to locate film in the space between "common sense" and "good sense."

The desire to use Gramsci to understand the complexities of film needs to start with an engagement with his ideas about "folklore." Before getting to the industrial machinery that we think of as Hollywood, Gramsci's notions of

folklore can help to locate the powerful relationship between dramatic storytelling and identity formation that cinema so completely perpetuates. And on the
other end of this account, we can consider how both Gramsci and "Hollywood"
become rearranged by the transformations of the digital media world.

GRAMSCI AND FOLKLORE

In his broad survey of the founders of folklore, Dundes (1999) included
Antonio Gramsci: "A political activist rather than a folklorist, Gramsci wrote
only a few passages in which he discussed folklore. But these few lines have
generated much controversy, perhaps out of proportion to their number.
Nevertheless, Gramsci deserves to be considered in any history of international folklorists" (p. 131). Dundes noted that Gramsci argued that folklore
needed to be studied as a conception of the world, a way of living life and
finding meaning that anchored the lives of the peasants and the proletariat,
that is, the "folk": the cultural group that Gramsci came from and was raised
in before the university education in Turin granted to him as a disadvantaged
student. The result of his becoming a political activist and intellectual in the
generally understood sense grounded him in the idea that being an intellectual
was a possibility for people from the subaltern classes. He later developed
this into his complex construction of the ideas of traditional intellectuals
educated in traditional institutions and of "organic" intellectuals who may or
may not have a formal education, but who remain products and members of
the subaltern class.

Gramsci believed that the oral knowledge that existed as folktales was an
important object of study. Since his larger goal was to empower members
of subaltern cultures to critically reflect on their own circumstances, an
understanding of folklore was a critical component of achieving critical self-
knowledge. As Dundes argued, Gramsci's attitude toward folklore appeared
somewhat ambivalent; its importance as an object of study also saw this folklore knowledge in relation to religious belief and superstition, which needed
to undergo critical scrutiny in order not to remain a source of oppression.
Gramsci (1992) saw much to argue against in this conception of folklore:

> It seems to me that until now folklore has been studied (in fact, until now,
> there has only been the collection of raw material) as a "picturesque" element.
> It ought to be studied as a "conception of the world" of particular social strata
> which are untouched by modern currents of thought. This conception of the
> world is not elaborated and systematized because the people, by definition, can-
> not do such a thing; and it is also multifarious, in the sense that it is a mechanical
> juxtaposition of various conceptions of the world, if it is not, indeed, a museum

of fragments of all the conceptions of the world and of life that have followed one another throughout history. Even modern thought and science furnish elements to folklore, in that certain scientific statements and certain opinions, torn from their context, fall into the popular domain and are "arranged" within the mosaic of tradition. (Pascarella's "Scoperta dell'America" shows how notions about Christopher Columbus and other figures, disseminated by elementary school textbooks, are assimilated in bizarre ways.) Folklore can be understood only as a reflection of the conditions of life of the people, although folklore frequently persists even after those conditions have been modified in bizarre combinations. (Gramsci, 1992, p. 186)

Folklore thus acts as a kind of cultural repository of residual knowledge and meaning that in many ways provides opposition to the "official" accounts of meaning, depending on the relationship between the official version offered by the state and the version arrived at through critical philosophy and science. As Gencarella (2010) asserted, the contemporary United States sees "many on the Right advocate religious instruction rather than science education; opposition to this agenda by the Left would remain consistent with Gramsci's critique of folklore" (p. 225). Gencarella also noted how Gramsci's take on folklore does not acknowledge that a reassertion of folkloric meanings would actually help subaltern groups. But Gramsci focused on the positive gains achieved through the replacement of folkloric meaning with meaning grounded in philosophy and science.

One important way of understanding the process of hegemony sees the negotiation between the oppressive regimes of power and the resistant responses grounded in folklore. Gramsci's notion of folklore described it as a body of knowledge that people take as the true account of things unless and until a critically focused education displaces it. This, of course, happens through a process that uses philosophy and science as critical tools to empower groups in a culture whose power is limited because of their hanging on to folklore, religion, and superstition.

Folklore consists of a variety of kinds of knowledge, including the collection of stories that a culture reproduces in the effort to maintain a conception of the world from one generation to the next. Superstitions are taught, fables of social instruction are told, and rituals and holidays are celebrated in the effort to maintain a culture over time. As Holub (2010) explained, in understanding folklore "Gramsci's analysis of civil society included the study of every possible piece of writing designed for readers, such as a parish newsletter, or a serial novel in a newspaper, precisely because civil society is constituted by multiple layers of 'intellectual functions'" (p. 16). This even happens when those sets of folklore instructions actually have the effect of political and social disempowerment for members of the group. And it even happens when the disempowered subject pays for the experience of reaffirming political realities. It is in this connection that we can talk about what happens when a mass media message—in the guise of a work of art—enters the age of mechanical reproduction. We know this as cinema.

THE HEGEMONY OF CONVENTION

Gramsci argued that the hegemonic process reflects a negotiation of values, where the interests of subaltern groups are partially formed through ideological institutions. The more formal reproduction takes place in educational institutions. The more informal aspect, and a major part of folklore, is expressed and reproduced through media. Arguably, the development of legacy media, like the film industry, has taken over much of the space that used to be taken up by oral folk traditions. Thus, the power to create and disseminate stories is moved into a system that is mechanized, guided by a "Fordist" approach to the production of storytelling, and privatized under a set of capitalist processes of profit. Under Gramsci's idea of "Fordism" (a term originating from the car manufacturer), workers are paid for the production of cars, and then are persuaded to desire and then buy what they played a small part in making. We can see a parallel in "Hollywoodism," which industrialized the production of popular culture material that would hegemonically feed the culture's construction of itself, while audiences paid for the privilege. Achieving the level of cultural dominance that we find reflected in the history of film requires additional levels of negotiation; the stories depicted would have to be desired enough that large numbers of people turn out and pay for the privilege of watching them, so that the large investment in the production process could turn a profit.

For film as a legacy form of folklore storytelling, the critical component was creating an experience that was desired by the masses. To get to that level of cultural dominance, filmmaking developed sets of conventions, which became critical to sustaining a paying audience. Quite early on, film drew on conventions of genre, theatricality, and storytelling to develop an approach to narrative that was easy to consume and played to the desire of mass audiences to be entertained.

Many of the initial experiments that make up the beginnings of film were dedicated to documenting small fragments of real life, such as the Lumiere Brothers' film *La Sortie de l'usine Lumiere a Lyon* ("Workers Leaving the Lumiere Factory"), which was shot and screened for an audience in March of 1895 in Paris. By November of that year, screenings in Berlin were charging admission, and the Lumieres had their first screening that charged admission in December of 1895. This included what historians believe was the first fictional narrative film, *L'Arroseur arose* ("Tables Turned on the Gardener"). It was a one-minute comedy.

The possibilities for the development of fictional narrative developed quickly in France, with the work of Alice Guy Blanche, who made *La fée aux choux* ("The Fairy of the Cabbages") in 1896. It is worth noting that Alice Guy Blanche was significant as a pioneering director, writer, and studio owner who deserves much more attention than she usually gets. She also is credited with what might have been the first all-African American cast film in 1912, after co-founding a film studio in New York and then expanding to New Jersey, in the period before Hollywood would arise as the dominant production center.

In addition to the roles that the Lumieres and Blanche played in the development of narrative fiction film, Georges Melies made the film "A Trip to the Moon" in 1902. The next year saw the production of the American Western "The Great Train Robbery," directed by Edwin S. Porter for the Edison Manufacturing Company. The film was a significant commercial success, and helped to solidify the notion that narrative fiction films were viable. Part of this viability resulted from the rapidly developing industrialization of a film production industry, but also in the deployment of accessible sets of conventions dictating how narrative fiction filmmaking would work.

As genres rapidly developed in those early decades, the new culture industry imported theatrical conventions, and a whole system of easily understood characters, recognizable actors, and identifiable genres developed. Audiences were being voluntarily educated into knowing what to expect when they paid to attend a film. At the center of narrative fiction was the power of the suspension of disbelief. Audience members, situated typically in the "fourth wall" position, viewed the narrative unacknowledged, though the acknowledgment was there in the way that the industry catered to them. The resulting profits provided the capital for the industry and its managers to go on to do more conventionally based storytelling.

The hegemonic power of these filmmaking conventions lies in how audiences learn them, and watch with a suspension of the idea that the people they watch onscreen are actors, that these stories are artificial constructions. The filmgoers are sutured into the narrative in a way that allows them to believe in the "reality" of the fiction being displayed in front of them, a way that is learned, familiar, and easy to consume. The parallel to Gramsci's notion of folklore is tangible in how it plays a role in the construction of the identity of the audience member, who is not so much a passive observer as a participant in the construction of a cultural reality, like a worker making Ford cars, enjoying the wages received, and using them to buy a Ford. For that to work, the worker does not have to be aware of the circularity of the process, and is "sold" on the freedom and independence that a car represents, even if the economic reality of the cycle would tell a different story. In the same way, audience members of what became the dominant Hollywood style of narrative fiction filmmaking learned what they needed to know without thinking critically about what it meant for the construction of their identities. Rather than the illusion of freedom that came with the car, the audiences for this dominant form of storytelling would experience the pleasures of popular culture without understanding the way myths were integrated into their sense of themselves and their culture.

These sets of conventions are like language in that they change over time in a somewhat organic way, in the same way that Gramsci described the changes in folklore that happened as a result of exposure to critical, philosophical, and scientific education (both formal and informal). Understanding the processes of convention as it changes over time requires a critical turn for both individuals and groups in a culture. This becomes most obvious when the representations of a group identity in film—a marginalized group identified through gender, race, or other identity marks—appear "conventionally" stereotypical or reductive. Some critics have suggested that the argument about hegemony is too functionalist and deterministic; for example, Gottdiener (1985) suggested that semiotics could rescue "hegemonists" from their determinism. But the Women's Movement and African American activist groups made a more significant case by arguing the problematics of conventional representations, and identifying a need to resist and renegotiate representations. Conventions are a question of coding and decoding (Hall, 1980), which happens at both an individual and group level.

This suggests that the sets of conventions produced through film serve as a site of cultural struggle if those conventions perpetuate ideas that become culturally problematic. That struggle may come from those on the political Right who argue that some conventions are morally problematic, and see them as toxic to young people who must be protected from them. The struggle also may come from the political Left, from groups who believe that the regime of conventions repeats destructive representations and reinforces racist, sexist, or homophobic ideas in the wider culture. These positions represent a kind of critical reflection on the power of the conventions laced through the media systems. They represent attempts on behalf of interest groups to question the "common sense" frameworks repeated through conventions and which move toward Gramsci's notion of "good sense."

HISTORICAL REPRESENTATION: MASSACRES IN FILM AND TELEVISION

Historical representations in media are sites of hegemonic struggle. Parallels occur in the ideological apparatus of education, such as the misrepresentation of history that might assert a unified patriotism rather than a critical perspective on history. This battle over textbook and public school content, as discussed by Zimmerman (2005), reflects the desire for broader representation of underrepresented groups in schooling. The work of Black activists over the last several decades has resulted in changes in the teaching of history to include Frederick Douglass and Martin Luther King, Jr.—but not without a hegemonic compromise:

> To be sure, the victory has never been complete. Jealously guarding their own dominant position in the American narrative, old-stock white conservatives worked to block immigrant and black voices from school textbooks. Eventually most parties to the dispute reached a rough compromise: each racial and ethnic group could enter the story, provided that none of them questioned the story's larger themes of freedom, equality, and opportunity. (Zimmerman, 2005, p. 4)

Experienced as unusual generational differences in history education, these kinds of "culture wars" parallel representations in popular media. The struggle over textbook content occurs on a parallel track with efforts to change the content—the conventions—of popular media toward both an inclusivity of group representations and corrections where the historical record becomes amended to include pieces of history that had suffered neglect, the product of intentional suppression. How could a story of a valiant American land of equality and freedom be reproduced if it included stories of enslaved peoples, settler colonialism, indigenous genocide, and imperial expansion?

Among the conventions of movies over the decades, representations that created easy points of access could only do so at the expense of critical reflection. Western films typically presented an imaginary of expansion across the continent as a struggle to "civilize" wild and untamed spaces. But these conventions needed a certain kind of single-minded adherence to the idea of history for the genre to work. In an article anticipating the rather colossal failure of the 2013 film version of *The Lone Ranger*—which included the casting of actor Johnny Depp (who claimed native ancestry, though it was never documented) as Tonto—*The Atlantic* included this commentary about the tradition of the Hollywood Western:

> The other great theme of the Western, after that of the conquering of native peoples and the establishment of civilization in the desert, is that of loss and of nostalgia for a certain way of life—the early freedoms of the West, the idea of riding across an unfenced landscape, the infinite possibilities of the frontier. That "West," of course, is already gone, fallen, conquered. It has been for decades, even though holding onto some sense of it seems crucial to our identity as Americans. Movie Westerns have been tracking that loss for a century. (Agresta, 2013)

The nostalgia for the Western described in Agresta's article reflects an awareness of the problematic kind of history interlaced in the conventions of the genre. The genocidal conquering of indigenous nations was simply a means to assert the value of frontier expansion as a motif in America's collective notion of its own identity, a motif certainly not shared by some indigenous communities, and certainly a way of noting that the past cannot stand up to critical scrutiny. Echoes of this history play out in other hegemonic struggles, like the attempts to eliminate Native Americans as mascots, the struggles to greenlight more Hollywood films written by, directed by, and starring members of native communities, and efforts to find a way to represent a history that acknowledges the racism and xenophobia at the core of these narrative conventions.

The damage of these conventions as they struggle through corrections parallel other struggles, as brilliantly observed by James Baldwin:

> I have to speak as one of the people who have been most attacked by the Western system of reality. It comes from Europe. That is how it got to America. It raises the question of whether or not civilizations can be considered equal, or whether one civilization has a right to subjugate—in fact, to destroy—another. . . . In the case of the American Negro, from the moment you are born every stick and stone, every face, is white. Since you have not yet seen a mirror, you suppose you are, too. It comes as a great shock around the age of 5, 6, or 7 to discover that the flag to which you have pledged allegiance, along with everybody else, has not pledged allegiance to you. It comes as a great shock to see Gary Cooper killing off the Indians, and although you are rooting for Gary Cooper, that the Indians are you. (1965, p. 32)

This commentary shows how the struggle over conventional representations works, starting with the initial identification with the "hero" on the screen, followed by a critical realization of what has gone wrong with this sense of one's self. But this is not just an individual realization; it is a realization that can reach broad cultural meanings, and encourage audiences to become Gramsci's intellectuals, to use the process of critical reflection for both realization of the circumstances of the individual, and the connections to the larger group struggle that focuses on power.

Baldwin pointed out the way that the experiences of the American Negro make sense in the face of the conventions of Western films at the time, yet need a great amount of critical self-awareness. In a Gramscian sense, this reflection on representation and film spectatorship becomes a representative anecdote of the larger possibilities that exist in an audience member who seeks a counterhegemonic sense of the meaning of a popular culture text. It poses the kind of intellectual activity that Gramsci saw as necessary for addressing the way a folklore-based understanding of the world is built without a critical take on the elements, and, to Baldwin's great credit, an insightful juxtaposition of the plight of indigenous peoples with the Black experience in America.

A similar, though more problematic, juxtaposition takes place in the controversial film *Soldier Blue* (1970). Directed by Ralph Nelson, the film presents a reversal of many of the tropes of the standard Western film. Set in Colorado Territory in 1877, it depicts a Union soldier left after a battle as one of two survivors, the other being a White woman who had lived with the Cheyenne. She works to get the soldier to understand the conflict from the native point of view, telling the soldier of his naïve attitude toward what is happening in this civilizing expansion of colonialism. Through a series of escalating conflicts between cultural ideologies, their movement through the territory leads them to fail in an attempt to stop a massacre of a peaceful Cheyenne village. In a scene of graphic violence, the U.S. Army slaughters the native group. The film depicted an account of the Sand Creek Massacre, where between 100 and 500 people were killed, the majority of them women and children.

The entertainment listings magazine *Time Out* criticized the film for its strange middle section that played out like a romance between the soldier and the woman, and accused the director of using the graphic depictions of the massacre just to generate more profit ("Soldier Blue," n.d.). However, if one were to watch the film without any additional reading, it would not be clear at first how the film was juxtaposing the Indian massacre with the American experience in Vietnam at the time. The year before the film's release, newspapers and television were full of reports of the My Lai Massacre, where U.S. troops killed between 300 and 500 unarmed civilians, including accounts of gang rape and the killing of young children.

Much like Baldwin coming to understand racism in the United States through Westerns, *Soldier Blue* offers a perspective on both indigenous genocide and U.S. wartime atrocities that completely contradict the nostalgia constructed within most Western conventions. The suspicion that these films were made only to make a profit is unquestioningly part of the reason they came into existence, but the possibility exists for their turning the "common sense" of a Western into Gramsci's notion of "good sense" that arises from critical reflection.

Such transformations occur outside of the genre of the Western as well, and have compelling positions that connect popular culture with historical knowledge. On Memorial Day weekend in 1921, a Black shoeshine worker in Tulsa, Oklahoma, was accused of assaulting a seventeen-year-old White female elevator operator. After his arrest, word traveled that he would be lynched, which brought out hundreds of White armed men; a group of seventy-five Black men, some of whom were armed, arrived at the same site to prevent the lynching. A conflict erupted. White rioters rampaged through the area known as the Greenwood district, also known as "Black Wall Street." An unknown number of Black citizens were killed, as stores were looted, Black-owned homes and businesses were burned, and the neighborhood was destroyed. According to the 2001 commission that was set up to investigate the event, between 75 and 300 people were killed, and 10,000 Black Tulsa residents were rendered homeless.

For many decades, the incident was not discussed in public, and the event was not included in the state's required Oklahoma history class. The event was gradually brought back into the public consciousness through books such as Rilla Askew's novel *Fire in Beulah* (2001) and Tim Madigan's nonfiction account *The Burning: Massacre, Destruction, and the Tulsa Race Riot of 1921* (2001). In 2000, the documentary *The Tulsa Lynching of 1921: A Hidden Story* aired on Cinemax. The name of the incident changed over time as consciousness of the event grew, from the Tulsa Race Riot to the Tulsa Race Massacre. In February of 2020, Jay Connor in *The Root* reported that the 1921 Tulsa Race Massacre would officially become part of the Oklahoma school curriculum, starting in the fall of 2020, while the school system would have to start the year contending with a massive COVID pandemic as well.

Arguably, the most significant transformation in the treatment of this tragedy had to do with the incident's depiction in two different series on HBO. In October 2019, the fantasy superhero series *Watchmen* premiered. It presented a remixed version of the 1986 comic series/graphic novel, and shifted attention to issues of race in its alternative history. Though mainly set in Tulsa in 2019, the series starts with a depiction of the Tulsa Massacre, showing the historically accurate use of firebombs dropped from airplanes flown by members of the White mob. The depiction in the series brought the 1921 Tulsa Massacre to the attention of a wider national and international audience. In the plot, the incident sets up the vast ongoing racial conflict between aggrieved Whites, who hold political and capital power, and Blacks, immigrants, and anyone not an aggrieved White person.

The other depiction of the massacre occurred in the horror series *Lovecraft Country*, which aired from August to October 2020. The series, mainly set in 1955, tells the story of Tic Freeman, a Black veteran of the Korean War, who returns home to his family on the south side of Chicago. He receives a letter from his missing father, which refers to a "family inheritance," suggesting he go to the town of Ardham, Massachusetts. Tic's uncle, who researches and writes a "Green Book"-style guide of safe places to go for Black travelers, goes with Tic and his friend Leti as they head to Ardham, and we are shown the harsh realities of the Jim Crow America of the 1950s. They are attacked by White racist cops but are saved by monsters out of a Lovecraftian story, amorphous monsters that tear apart the cops. These elements of the series show a world of magic and supernatural forces juxtaposed over the realities of White supremacy. As the series tells an interlocking series of stories set in this world, eventually Tic, Leti, and Tic's rescued father, Montrose, use a "multiverse machine" to travel back to Tulsa in 1921 to rescue a book that would allow them to reverse a curse and save Diana, Tic's young cousin. Diana had been turned into a monstrously exaggerated version of Topsy, an enslaved child from *Uncle Tom's Cabin*, but in a demonic form through a curse placed on her by a racist cop who uses magic. The book had originally been destroyed during the Tulsa Massacre, so they arrive the day the massacre takes place. They are eventually able to get the book from the ancestors of Tic's mother.

In *Lovecraft Country*, we see a prosperous Black community in Tulsa as it becomes destroyed in the massacre. Like the depiction in *Watchmen*, the violence of the White mob leads to indiscriminate racial murder. Brueggeman (2019) discussed how both depictions of the Tulsa Massacre point out how the act was perpetrated by communities of Whites:

> The scenes of Tulsa demonstrate something important: the role of a white community in slaughtering a Black community. I have written before about the importance of implicating White communities in Black trauma. . . .When it comes to the depiction of the racial violence, the focus on White communal participation is essential. This is especially true for discussing Tulsa. The Tulsa Massacre was not the result of a few bad apples. It was the result of a rotten orchard. . . . *The Watchmen* portrayed the diversity of perpetrators with imagery. In one scene, viewers watch robed Klansmen seconds from killing an unarmed Black man. In another moment, killers are dressed in normal clothing. The show demonstrates that during this massacre the Klan and "everyday men" collaborated in the murders. In this scene, it is impossible to differentiate between the Klansmen and other White men. They are all murderers. *Lovecraft Country* took this a step further with their portrayal of the White community in Tulsa by including a White woman as a perpetrator.

These depictions offer disturbing, powerful images from pieces of filmic stories that offer a correction to the record of gaps in the historical record. They give audiences a different version of that past, a past that historical accounts pointedly repressed, whether one looks at the absence of attention in formal education of the history of Oklahoma, or other historical records that downplay the history.

From a Gramscian perspective, we can draw two important points from these depictions of a historical event. First, the "folklore" of this history of Oklahoma must change as a result of new knowledge, along with acknowledgment that other atrocities of racial violence, buried and removed from historical consciousness, likely occurred. Second, the popular distribution of these historical corrections is powerful because of the impact that legacy media, like film and streaming cable series, can have.

We need to keep in mind that both of these depictions appear in highly manipulative fictional frameworks. *Watchmen*'s premise offers an alternative history in which the Nixon administration did not fall into scandal, the United States won the Vietnam War (as the result of great atrocities), and Robert Redford became president in a world where people drive electric cars and cell phones do not exist. *Lovecraft Country* suggests that magic exists in the "real" world—and people use it not only to support White supremacy but also to change the race of a person from Black to White, defeat horrible curses, and suggest the potential of eternal life. Both *Watchmen* and *Lovecraft Country* sparked a critical popular conversation about what happened in Tulsa in 1921, an event most often accompanied by shock that this real-world historical atrocity was never in the history books, and not part of the popular memory.

So there is virtue that arises in how these depictions can change the body of knowledge in circulation in a culture. This knowledge becomes part of the anti-hegemonic struggle of people to identify, understand, and re-create their material circumstances. In this sense, by instigating further conversation about the historical circumstances surrounding the Tulsa Massacre, these two television series steer their audiences toward becoming Gramsci's organic intellectuals. The viewer who pursues a deeper understanding of Tulsa in 1921, or the Sand Creek Massacre of 1864, or the My Lai massacre of 1968, or any number of other historical events vital to the understanding of the full picture of a nation or culture, might turn to sources like Howard Zinn and his *A People's History of the United States* (1980). But the Gramscian mark of the organic intellectual has to do with what one does with the anti-hegemonic new knowledge. Gramsci argued that organic intellectuals are clear about their cultural associations, and seek to spread the word among the groups with whom they associate.

INTELLECTUALS IN MEDIA

Is it possible that reading films and television programs as expressing anti-hegemonic meanings through stories that focus on racism and xenophobia gives them too much credit? On the one hand, if we assume that there are organic intellectuals in media industries who are making films, TV, and streaming cable series, then it would certainly confirm the success of their efforts to communicate arguments about subaltern subject positions on a grand scale. On the other hand, if the goal is to not move the needle in terms of resistance against hegemony, these works may simply act as a pressure release, offering a momentary exploration of racism, sexism, and homophobia without really accomplishing a significant change in the struggle between cooperation and coercion. It certainly would be difficult to make the case that advances in technology, economics, and regulation, which have so fundamentally re-ordered access and distribution, have resulted in a less centralized corporate media environment.

A Gramscian perspective to cultural production allows for the possibility for alternative discourses that give voice to other groups who were usually consumers but not creators. As Hanno Hardt (1992) put it,

> the emergence of an alternative discourse in an atmosphere of participatory intellectual leadership thrives on a Gramscian understanding of intellectual work as involvement in the collective practice of producing and sharing knowledge. Thus, the diversity and quality of theoretical insights gained through retracing the hermeneutic tradition of European thought, and the impact of Western Marxism and feminism on contemporary social theory, have influenced these joint intellectual tasks of formulating theoretical propositions and research projects. (p. 214)

While Hardt focused on the possibilities for traditional intellectual projects, he also suggested that alternative discourses have the potential to widen the scope of resistance through popular media.

One important characteristic of media production in television, film, and other legacy visual media is their collaborative nature. They represent the work of collections of people in the media industries working in collaboration; these collections of people range from the projects of a scant few to spectacular productions representing the work of hundreds. Granted, many of these participants may work more on the technical side than the conceptual, but there are still large numbers of "above the line" people working in collaboration to make these media.

What people do when they consume media poses a related set of intellectual practices. For example, depictions of the Tulsa Massacre in *Watchmen* and *Lovecraft Country* led to a widespread response of the recognition of how formal education and the cultural paradigm frame gaps in history. The discussions that followed this awareness led to conversations about the significance of historical lacunae, as Fenwick (2020) wrote in the *New York Times*:

> The massacre lay hidden for decades. Educators did not teach it. Government offices did not record it. Even archival copies of some newspaper accounts were selectively expunged. On Monday, though, forensic investigators broke ground at the possible site of a mass grave in Oaklawn Cemetery, a few blocks from where much of the carnage occurred. . . . "There was a curtain of silence drawn to keep this quiet," said Scott Ellsworth, a Tulsa historian who wrote a history

of the massacre, "Death in a Promised Land: The Tulsa Race Riot of 1921." The
dig defies the official silence, he said, which was an attempt to hide the crime.

The point of these discussions wasn't just the light brought to the incident,
but the questions people asked as their awareness grew: Why did I not know
about this? Why was I not taught this? Why is it not part of the media world?
This interrogation of the culture leads to legitimate organic intellectual activity, which has since included efforts by people connected with the Black
Lives Matter movement to strongly encourage self-education, people to find
reading and viewing lists online, and to provide resources that might answer
some of those profound questions about the gaps in our collective representations of history. The means of distribution for this material brings attention
to the way digital and online networking has transformed our experiences as
producers and consumers—for better, and often for worse.

HEGEMONY IN VISUAL MEDIA

The significance of Hollywood's visual way of telling stories, including its
industrial production practices and the kinds of narrative fiction stories it
tells, makes up part of the story of U.S. cultural hegemony as both an internal
struggle and as a global phenomenon. The challenge within the U.S. media
system, as Artz and Murphy argued (2000), is the ability of the industries of
popular culture to respond to anti-hegemonic work through a combination of
efforts. These industries continue to produce work that reasserts the coercive
elements of the state and corporate value system, and, at the same time, work
to co-opt anti-hegemonic expressions. Artz and Murphy explained how hegemony operates on issues of Black American culture:

> Mass culture provides us with representations of black life that adhere to
> popular stereotypes and simultaneously allow black appreciation. The culture
> industries that control the production and distribution of movies and television
> rely on black cultural practices and productions for many of their creative inspi-
> rations, thus encouraging and to some extent subsidizing black culture, albeit on
> hegemonic terms. (p. 151)

These hegemonic terms mean a general resistance to a proportional level of
representation in popular culture texts. Artz and Murphy concluded that the
struggle between hegemony and counterhegemony follows the conditions in
which a subordinated group finds itself:

> In the context of satisfied needs and unappealing alternatives, hegemony can
> construct reasonable explanations for predominate social and cultural practices. A

counterhegemony does not develop without regard for the conditions confronting interconnected subordinate groups and individuals. In other words, a counterhegemony cannot even be conceived in a society where subordinate needs and interests are adequately met. Conversely, an existing hegemony will likely be challenged to the degree that material, political, and cultural conditions fail to meet subordinate interests and demands. In most instances, neither extreme exists. (p. 301)

Film and television frequently offered pleasures that to some extent satisfy the desire for entertaining storytelling, and the ability of film and television producers in the United States to produce and reproduce these narrative forms, and to learn how to export them around the world, led to a hegemonic dominance of U.S. popular culture throughout the world.

This reached a level where cultures were in the position of having to use regulation to maintain screen space for their own domestic production, so as not to completely see their media industries implode. UNESCO's (2005) "Convention on the Protection and Promotion of the Diversity of Cultural Expression" serves as an example of this. As explained by De Beukelaer et al. (2015):

The disputes within GATT and later WTO parties led to the statement of what is called "cultural exception"—a statement that free trade does not touch upon cultural products in the way of the other trade commodities. . . . The representatives of the EU, France, and Canada, in particular, formulated the rationality for this exception: cultural products and expressions should be treated differently than others, because they are of special significance for the countries and their national identities. . . .This led to the allowance of bilateral and multilateral agreements between European countries—also with some other countries—in different cultural industry sectors, particularly television and films. Import of high-budget US cinema and TV productions was restricted in the name of supporting European productions. This was linked to the promotion of global cultural diversity through facilitating the distribution of small productions without massive advertising and distribution means. (pp. 3–4)

The fundamentally destabilizing effects of the digital media environment also have affected these patterns of hegemony. The legacy media industries—traditions in film, television, photography, radio, and journalism—maintain their position at the center of the culture, still banking on an audience willing to pay for these more traditional "mass" media experiences for their entertainment and information. But changes in digital technology have changed the definition of these media. The boundaries have been destabilized between, for example, the formal idea of cinema and the idea of television, or the formal notion of radio and the formal notion of podcast content. This destabilization became particularly significant in the film industry as it tried to craft alternative distribution mechanisms in light of the 2020 and 2021 COVID crisis. Traditional theatrical distribution was severely marginalized, causing studios to consider direct and simultaneous streaming distribution (Premium Video on Demand, or PVoD). Additionally, media distribution across and around geographic boundaries exists in a state of flux, depending on the way networked connections change with varying levels of disregard for national boundaries.

One may have the sense that Gramsci anticipated a similar kind of transformation in his time. His understanding of arts and culture was being informed by a moment when there were fears that cinema might displace traditional performing arts, including the theatre and opera. In 1916, he wrote of this while working as a theatre critic for *Avanti!*:

> They say that the cinema is killing the theatre. . . .There would seem to be some basis to the sad observation that the audience's taste as degenerated and that bad times are round the corner for theatre. We, however, are thoroughly convinced that these complaints are founded on a jaded aestheticism and can easily be shown to depend on a false assumption . . . the cinema offers exactly the same sensations as the popular theatre, but under better conditions, without the choreographic contrivances of a false intellectualism, without promising too much while delivering little . . . the theatrical firms and companies will eventually realize that they need to change tack if they want to stay in being. (Gramsci, 2012, pp. 54–55)

Gramsci was writing at a time, of course, when films were still silent, and he mentions that a cinema audience member's attention was focused on movement rather than sound. He was sensitive not just to differences in the content between theatre and cinema, but also to the formal elements that change the experience from one form to another. Keeping in mind his desire to understand the way audiences were shifting, he was attentive to the aesthetics and politics of the media choices that they were making.

This issue later becomes clearer when Gramsci, in part of Notebook 23 written in 1934, wrote about the desires that motivate audiences to seek out film, theatre, and cultural expression broadly:

> It seems evident that, to be precise, one should speak of a struggle for a "new culture" and not for a "new art" (in the immediate sense). To be precise, perhaps it cannot even be said that the struggle is for a new artistic content apart from form because content cannot be considered abstractly, in separation from form. To fight for a new art would mean to fight to create new individual artists, which is absurd since artists cannot be created artificially. One must speak of a struggle

for a new culture, that is, for a new moral life that cannot but be intimately connected to a new intuition of life, until it becomes a new way of feeling and seeing reality and, therefore, a world intimately ingrained in "possible artists" and "possible works of art." (Gramsci, 2012, p. 98)

Gramsci's thoughts about cinema versus theatre were an early version of his idea that the audiences for these dramas were struggling for a new culture, represented by new mediated experiences, which become the foundation for a revised way of seeing and feeling reality. Analyzing changes like these can make for a complicated search, since it becomes so easy to substitute the cause and the effect. Is a film with a counterhegemonic meaning acting as a cultural cause to further the resistance to a hegemony? Or does it appear as a result of organic intellectuals responding to the coercive side of a hegemony, and finding a new way to, say, advance the conversation?

CONCLUSION

Gramsci, who had been trained as a linguist, understood the connection between language and the cultural reality that individuals and groups use to make sense of the world. He argued that folklore, expressed and repeated in language, should be studied seriously as a bridge across different parts of culture, and not reduced to quaint stories that should be disregarded:

> It is clear that, in order to achieve the desired end, the spirit of folklore studies should be changed, as well as deepened and extended. Folklore must not be considered an eccentricity, an oddity or a picturesque element, but as something very serious and is to be taken seriously. Only in this way will the teaching of folklore be more efficient and really bring about the birth of a new culture among the broad popular masses, so that the separation between modern culture and popular culture of folklore will disappear. (Gramsci, 2012, p. 191)

The separation that Gramsci described invites a comparison with the "folklore" that a culture acquires through legacy media like film and television, and online and streaming visual media. Often those media texts, the theatrical films, television series, and streamed storytelling, are consumed as entertainment, rather than being taken seriously as an object of study in popular culture.

But when we do look seriously at the content, we find contentious expressions that range from stories that support and perpetuate the hegemonic regime to texts that offer counterhegemonic arguments for thinking about the reality of the world where people find themselves. Gramsci's impulse to take folklore seriously directly parallels the imperative of media literacy to take the texts of popular culture seriously. The production of texts that use folkloric stories or elements is revised to align with existing ideologies of capitalism, patriarchy, and consumerism. The consumption of these texts contributes to the identities that are formed individually and collectively, through a complex combination of fictional fantasy and the visualization of blunt truths. This has been the power of drama and storytelling for as long as there has been storytelling and acting.

And buried within this idea of taking popular culture seriously, audiences—whether professional or organic intellectuals—are exposed to different arguments about history. The arguments do not specify how they are advancing a preferred take on history and discounting alternative stories. Consider the arguments for a thoroughly patriotic kind of civics education, tied to attempts to minimize the experiences of enslaved people or indigenous communities who suffered at the hands of settler colonialists. One need only look at the Pulitzer Prize-winning series of essays published by *The New York Times Magazine* as "The 1619 Project" (2019). The attempt to fill in a historical record of the experiences of Black Americans drew a major backlash; it even resulted in a report published by the 1776 Commission in the last days before the inauguration of President Joe Biden on January 18, 2021. The commission was dissolved and the report was removed from the White House website on January 20, 2021. Still accessible in the National Archives, the report was considered by many historians to be a whitewashing of the history of racial discrimination, instead asserting American Exceptionalism, and was written without any contact with professional U.S. historians. It stands, however, as an example (however poorly executed) of a desire to advance a selective hegemonic idea of history, and an attempt to suppress the kind of historical perspective that "The 1619 Project" was struggling to advance.

Within these stories that offer potential resistance to hegemony, we find constructions of identity that shape our notions of ourselves. Popular culture storytelling includes elements of representation that tell its audience what particular identity characteristics mean, and does so by displaying and exploring how power is distributed and negotiated. While this chapter has used examples from film and television to discuss issues of race and historical storytelling, there is much to be said from a Gramscian point of view about the way gender identity is expressed in our most popular fiction. In the following chapter, we suggest that we take seriously how entertainment film texts both reinforce and challenge elements of the hegemonic moment.

Chapter 4

Hegemonic Masculinity in the Mass Media

Gramsci's concern with the popular arts and their composite role as a vehicle for conveying a culture's ideologies not only encompasses the ways in which values and practices become reflected in cultural products such as plays and films but extends to notions about the proper behaviors and accepted ways of simply being. His engagement in theatre criticism provides us with a perspective of examining entertainment as disguised conduits for propaganda. Dombroski (1986) explained that Gramsci saw the theatre as a regulator of the social order: "The most popular plays of his time, written and staged to satisfy the tastes of the middle class, function ideologically to preserve the status quo and produce consensus" (p. 101). Because Gramsci aimed to find a way to empower the working class—those outside the structures of power—so it would become the hegemonic force required for radical prosocial change, he saw the theatre, and, by extension, the mass media, as a means for wider societal movement toward the just and equitable society envisioned by socialism.

Cultural producers of entertainment, whose existence relies on profit-making and who thus must take into consideration the tastes and preferences of their audiences, nonetheless can provide a means to allay the pressures of daily life, though temporarily, and even inspire viewers to action. Cultural products also hold the power to either uphold and reinforce hegemonic thought or challenge it outright. They can even manage to do both. Given the push and pull between dominant ideology and alternative ideologies that characterize hegemonic struggle, the teaching of media literacy requires a critical examining of popular entertainment, not only to uncover how today's media entertainment sphere assists in the maintenance work of keeping hegemony running but also to find ways to wedge into movies, television shows, and other seemingly non-ideological media artifacts the moral content that

67

Gramsci argued was needed in order for social change and progress to occur (Dombroski, 1986).

"Popular culture absorbs oppositional ideology, adapts it to the contours of the core hegemonic principles, and domesticates it; at the same time, popular culture is a realm for the expression of forms of resistance and oppositional ideology," observed Gitlin (1987, p. 242). Thus, entertainment media certainly can entertain, but they also hold the dual power to maintain the "establishment" *and* to forward the already-in-place alternatives and progressive ideas, ways of life, and behaviors experienced by the people in their everyday lives. In short, even as we mentioned in chapter 1 that society tends to be ahead of what the "record" of culture may contain in forms such as the cinema, television, and theatre, the media hold the potential to concretely sway people to let go of conventional wisdom and "common sense" and embrace good sense. All of this becomes possible when cultural producers *themselves* think creatively within the structural bindings of media economics to infuse their stories, however fantastical or seemingly mundane, with an ethical and moral consciousness on behalf of the people. Gramsci's vision for the arts, which are particularly created for and received and enjoyed by everyone, serves as the reason why popular culture offers such a rich platform not only for finding out how common sense and hegemonic ideas become emplaced but also for detecting counterhegemonies and resistance.

An aspect of culture is gender ideology, conveyed through socialization, personal experience, and, of course, the mass media. Gramsci (1971) himself addressed gender ideology and its role in the attainment of an ethical social order, famously writing that women needed to gain "genuine independence in relation to men" and see themselves in a new way regarding sexual relations (p. 587). While Slaughter (2011) posited that Gramsci could be viewed as holding feminist views, Liguori (2015) pointed out that his views on women based on how he wrote to his wife would be considered today as "macho" or "patriarchal" (p. 128). Indeed, Ledwith (2009) asserted, "He made an immense contribution to feminism without 'getting it'; such is the elusive nature of power and domination" (p. 686).[1]

Hegemony offers a fitting and germane way to examine and explain gendered power relations (Kenway, 2001); its relevance to the study of gender becomes even more significant when considering the nature of patriarchy as hegemonic and a function of consent, whether tacit or not. "In this sense, the production of gender differences becomes a critical point of gender struggle and reproduction, the site of gender control," argued Arnot (1982). "In addition to his work on the state, the most obvious connection between Gramsci's writings and women might seem those aspects which are related to popular culture and ideology" (p. 19).

In this chapter, we approach how Gramsci relates to the study of media and gender by examining popular culture as a conveyance of gender ideology. As a way to analyze how gender is controlled in society through popular culture, we start by reviewing definitions of contemporary masculinity, especially forms that have become commonsense ways of ascertaining fulfillment of the male role. First, we define what hegemonic masculinity entails, and how it aligns with Gramscian thought regarding certain ideas about appropriate and desired behaviors of males, particularly in a generalized U.S. culture. The qualities associated with proper "manhood" and the implications of a strict adherence to certain forms of masculinities that enforce gender difference are discussed, followed by a review of hegemonic masculinity research of media forms. In chapter 5, we present a textual analysis of a U.S.-made media artifact that has found historic, international success, and how its portrayals of masculinity both uphold hegemonic thought regarding gender relations and present counterhegemonic behaviors that push against that status quo ideal by incurring feminine-associated traits.

HEGEMONIC MASCULINITY

The concept of hegemonic masculinity, formulated in the 1980s and emergent of women's studies and its feminist foundations, applies Gramscian hegemony to an understanding of how social institutions perpetuate the construction of the male role; it is a feminist approach to the study of masculinity (Connell & Messerschmidt, 2005).[2] There is not one singular, universal masculinity, because it is culturally dependent; across cultures, what it means to "be man" differs. Furthermore, within a culture, or a multicultural society, multiple masculinities (i.e., gender performance expected by males) may exist, noted Connell (2001), with hegemonic masculinity referring to the culturally dominant form in a given setting. A dominant masculinity ideology thus "defines the social norms for the male gender role" (Levant, 2011, p. 768).

As we discussed in chapter 1, power at the level of civil society is wielded indirectly through the enforcement of cultural norms and practices. The unwritten rules of gendered behavior function this way, with socialization to the appropriate ways of "being" serving as a way to maintain sexual difference. The hegemonic form of masculinity thus "signifies a position of cultural authority and leadership, not total dominance; other forms of masculinity persist alongside," explained Connell (2001, p. 17). Connell noted that the hegemonic form within a culture tends to be highly visible and emulated— even though performing it may not be attainable by most of the men within that culture. For instance, exemplars of masculinity, such as sports stars, serve as "symbols of authority" for behavioral aspirations associated with maleness, even though most boys and men do not live up to them (Connell & Messerschmidt, 2005, p. 846).

The socially created dichotomy of masculinity versus femininity serves as an important way that gender roles, expectations, and performance remain in place; one is either masculine or feminine. Androgyny, the amalgam of an individual's traits considered both masculine and feminine, continues in contemporary times to be marginalized, especially in patriarchal societies. Thus, hegemonic masculinity exists only in opposition to femininity and non-hegemonic masculinities; its hegemonic characterization is achieved mainly through "cultural ascendancy—discursive persuasion—encouraging all to consent, coalesce around, and embody such unequal relations between men and women, between masculinity and femininity, and among masculinities" (Messerschmidt, 2018, p. 28).

Masculinities are social performances, enacted in the practices of daily life; they become part of a culture's collective mindset. Patterns of behavior linked to one's gender (with gender the socially constructed identity associated with one's sex) are conducted at the level of the individual and defined by institutions (Connell, 2001). Thus, hegemonic masculinities (and femininities) result from the social learning by a culture's membership. The discursive persuasion mentioned by Messerschmidt (2018) relates directly to the portrayals of masculine performance in mass media. Not only is masculine identity "taught, performed, and disciplined," argued Wooden and Gillam (2014), but the depiction of gender as seen in cultural products should obviously be considered as influential, with mainstream U.S. media serving for children as a "'public school' for maintaining ideological hegemony" (p. xvii). While the role repertoires of masculinity—however performed in whatever cultural settings—fluctuate and change over time and between public and private realms of interaction, mass media reflective of a particular culture play a role in regulating what masculinity means (Roublou, 2009, citing others). And, of course, even across the media landscape the hegemonic struggle between upholding "traditional" notions of manhood and resistant portrayals signifies that what it means to be a man does not follow a single formula.

Boon (2005), writing about the paradox of mythic masculinity in Western culture as an "unattainable ideal," offered this description of still-held notions of manhood: "Bravery and violence in men are still venerated, and, in general, overt displays of emotional sensitivity and aversion to pain in men are still disdained" (p. 308). Cultural ideas about manhood being all about toughness and strength have real consequences, noted prominent gender educator and scholar Jackson Katz (2020), particularly when leadership continues to be associated with versions of masculinity that emulate those traits. Katz pointed out that violence, or threat of its use, is a tactic used by men unable to achieve their goals otherwise. The connection between violence, power, and masculinity also relates to domestic violence in intimate relationships as well as larger issues of gender, he explained. Kenway (2001) previously had noted that violence serves as one basis of patriarchal power; this recurrent element of masculinity is connected to certain values and behaviors upheld by societal structures and institutions. Connell (2001) pointed to video games in particular as a conduit for stereotyped behaviors that link violence to masculinity.

"To be masculine, for most contemporary Americans, means to be strong, fearless, self-assertive—to face down danger," wrote Wade and Bridges (2020). Connell also listed the practical reasons for why looking at masculinity in particular is important: the toxic effects implicated by the adherence to following the (socially mandated) rules of contemporary masculinities, which include adverse effects on health, as well as the risk of injury, victimization, racism, violence against women, and homophobic violence. Regarding the latter, the policing of heterosexuality is a major theme in hegemonic masculinity (Connell & Messerschmidt, 2005).

Just as the concept of masculinity as ideology requires the caveat that ideals regarding manhood vary (Levant, 2011), the term "hegemonic masculinities" more accurately describes the hegemonic form of masculinity predominant at varying levels of culture (e.g., micro-local, such as in individual schools, or regional, national, and global). However, one can argue that there tends to be forwarded in various media forms some common elements that define masculinity repeatedly and widely. In U.S. American culture, for example, idealized manhood is associated with traits such as strength, self-sufficiency, invulnerability, and emotional control (Johnson, 1997). Traditional norms associated with masculinity in contemporary U.S. culture include differentiation from femininity, never showing weakness, being respected for achievement success, dominance, extreme self-reliance, and restrictive emotionality (Levant, 2011).

The overriding mandate that men not be like women in any way, lest the gender order be threatened, or, more drastically, eliminated altogether, manifests in the socialization of boys and young men to avoid appearing vulnerable, scared, or simply a normal human being who expresses feelings in the way girls and women are "allowed" to (though not wholly without their own negative consequences). Masculine credibility is established through violence, while so-called "feminine" traits are not only eschewed but discouraged and even serve as a source for punishment: "Qualities like compassion, caring, empathy, intellectual curiosity, fear, vulnerability, even love—basic human qualities that boys have inside them every bit as much as girls do—get methodically driven out of them by a sexist and homophobic culture," Katz explained in his 2013 documentary *Tough Guise 2*. When boys and men do exhibit these qualities, he further explicated, they are labeled "unmanly," "feminine," and "unwomanly"; the heterosexual policing associated with hegemonic masculinity becomes manifest when such qualities also are called "gay." What results, according to Katz, is that boys are taught to avoid any semblance of appearing as the "other" gender. This not only inhibits individual growth and development but serves as an impediment to cultural change that would make way for gender egalitarianism in wider society.

The stereotype of the "strong, silent" man does not fall far from the ideal of traditional masculinity, at least the masculinity that permeates culture to the degree of still being considered the most typical ideal. To explain a tendency among men in his clinical practice to be unable to describe their emotions through words, Ronald F. Levant proposed the normative male alexithymia hypothesis in the early 1990s. The concept of normative male alexithymia, which associates a particular gender with alexithymia—a term meaning "without words for emotions"—described "a socialized pattern of restrictiveness emotionality influenced by traditional masculinity ideology" (2011, p. 772). Levant theorized that due to strict gender socialization that followed traditional masculinity ideals during childhood, young males "did not develop a vocabulary for, or an awareness of, many of their emotions" (p. 772), with the greatest deficits stemming from the inability or disallowance for expressing feelings of vulnerability, sadness, and fear.[3] Further, the avoidance of appearing weak (the oft-heard "boys don't cry" mandate) becomes associated with the discouragement to exhibit expressions of caring, fondness, and feelings of attachment to others, according to Levant. Thus, openly showing love to family members, not to mention friends, thus implies weakness, or, worse, femininity. Coupled with the strict policing of heterosexuality, verbally and nonverbally showing affection to male friends thus contributes to the fears that Katz identified—of boys and men being derided for not only feeling but demonstrating affection, especially in public.

The maintenance of social order depends on ensuring one does not deviate from the socially constructed ideals of gender identity for fear of not appearing sufficiently masculine (or, for women, feminine), as explained by Johnson (1997). Threats to one's gender identity—and to one's status as a man within a patriarchy—can result in negative consequences that can not only damage the individual, but also reverberate throughout wider society. The containment of individual expression and the confinement to certain behaviors that result from enforcement of gender boundaries illustrate the power of hegemonic thought in civil society. Boon (2005) alluded to this when explaining the pervasiveness of masculine ideals as encapsulated in Western examples of culturally created heroic male exemplars: Men are "unable to escape the demands of the hero figure without abnegating their masculinity and thus sacrificing the silent approbation of culture, yet often drawn by a sense of justice toward renunciation of masculinity" (p. 309).

Though still waiting to become a positive hegemony, progressive viewpoints regarding the male role—such as nurturing children, equal participation in housework, and openly communicating one's feelings—have put pressure on men. This led to confusion about how to correctly perform manhood, resulting in a "masculinity crisis" since the 1990s, according to Levant (2011). Levant saw the interrogation of traditional norms of masculinity as providing a framework for "positive new visions for how to be a man in today's world, visions that could support the optimal development of men, women, and children" (p. 766).

Hegemonic masculinity does not exist without a socially created difference between the masculine and the feminine. However, hegemonic femininity does not mean the opposite of hegemonic masculinity, nor does it relate to a dominant version of those traits considered "feminine" as opposed to being "masculine"—such as nurturing, being submissive, or being "nice" (Fixmer-Oraiz & Wood, 2019). Hegemonic femininity, rather, refers to a dominant ideology that characterizes what is considered "womanliness"; Ussher (1997) listed three components of hegemonic femininity: having and pursuing physical beauty, heterosexual sex, and interest in romance. These "pursuits" expected of women and often used in advertising appeals—such as for beauty products that make a female person look younger or prettier, or make her successful at attracting a man (the heterosexual sex and interest in romance elements)—create a common sense that dictates if a woman is not interested in looking attractive or wearing makeup, or if her goal in life excludes marriage to a man, then she is not feminine.

The study of gender becomes useful for the creation of knowledge and has a "purely intellectual purpose," wrote Connell (2001), and to examine masculinity in particular, and its hegemonic iterations and the ways they become communicated through media "illuminates the lives of men and the forms and dynamics of masculinities" (p. 25). Kenway (2001) noted that the widespread acceptance of hegemonic masculinity demonstrates a major legacy of Gramsci's thought in educational studies. Although the term hegemonic masculinity may imply a single, monolithic version of masculinity, one must remember that more than one kind of masculinity may exist within a given culture or society, because masculinity can be performed differently depending on the situational context in which such behavior is expected or emulated. However, when referring to the continued presence of a common version of masculinity in a generalized way, such as in the wider U.S. American culture in a national-culture sense, we use the term hegemonic masculinity here to refer to the highly visible, composite traits associated with manhood most commonly depicted in cultural products and displayed in societal attitudes and the descriptors masculinity studies scholars use to describe the prevailing conception of manhood in contemporary U.S. American and Western culture.

MEDIATED MASCULINITY

Media representations of masculinity have long been examined, with scholarly treatments that analyze the content of a range of media forms providing evidence of recurrent themes regarding the portrayal of men. For example, Rehling (2009) deconstructed a range of films from the 1990s and early 2000s featuring "ordinary" White, heterosexual male characters. Rehling identified thematic commonalities of films with similar narratives and presentations of the male body. For example, popular movies starring muscularized characters (such as those depicted in the films of Sylvester Stallone and Arnold Schwarzenegger) symbolize "white phallic power" (p. 4), and films about disenfranchised, disgruntled White men, such as 1999's *Fight Club*, address White male victimhood. By analyzing media representations of an ordinary form of male identity (White, heterosexual masculinity), which represents an ideological and political dominance challenged during a time of identity politics, Rehling's purpose was to reveal this hegemonic form of masculinity is "a volatile category that can only be stabilized through reiteration" (p. 3).

Hegemonic masculinity in particular serves as a theoretical foundation for studies examining media coverage of notable male celebrities. For example, Trujillo (1991) relied on the concept of hegemonic masculinity to approach the way print news articles and television ads portrayed a U.S. sports star, major league baseball player Nolan Ryan. Trujillo identified how descriptions of Ryan matched cultural tropes that linked certain persona traits typical of the U.S. American version of manhood, notably, physical strength; workplace success and achievement (breadwinner role); fatherhood performance; and "cowboy," the idealized rural, risk-taking frontiersman. Basically fulfilling every manly role connected to "American" cultural ideology, Ryan's mediated masculinity aligned with a hegemonic masculinity that unquestioningly accepts a proper and correct version of being a man. Key here is the mediated version of Ryan, rather than the actual version of the person himself, whose portrayal as a model father relied on news coverage of how he enacted that role publicly with his two sons, but not his daughter. Trujillo's analysis identified the components of mythic masculinity in media portrayals of an actual male person, who nevertheless became almost over-idealized to the point that one could imagine him to be a fictional character.

Vavrus (2002) examined hegemonic masculinity as revealed in television news accounts of stay-at-home fathers. Although legitimating "feminine" traits of nurturance and the task of childcare as properly masculine, these stories about men who engage in gender role reversal may have contributed to a revised image of masculinity. However, narratives of the "Mr. Mom" (the title of a 1983 film about a man who becomes a househusband after losing his job) also made clear that these were still "real men" who continued to engage in masculine-typed behaviors, such as playing sports with their children. Praised as progressive and endorsed by childcare experts, the demographic considerations of White, heterosexual dads, and the reaffirmation of their manhood credentials provide reassurance of a gender status quo and reinforce traditional masculinity, the normalcy of the nuclear family, and heteronormativity. Vavrus's study of media depictions of actual stay-at-home fathers provides documentation of the newsworthiness of new conceptions about fatherhood and masculinity.

Around the same time as Vavrus's study on role-reversal dads in the news, Connell (2001) assessed such reports of social change as not reflective of actual behavior by stating, "Much of this talk turns out to be fantasy; most men have little interest in changing patterns of child care and housework" (p. 22). Social discourse, such as feature stories in the news, may give the appearance of movement away from traditional masculinity and toward fathers' increasing participation in childcare. Pew survey data show that in the United States, while time devoted to childcare among fathers may have increased between the 1960s and 2010s, from an average of 2.5 hours per week in 1965 to 8 hours per week in 2016, it is still far less than that of mothers, whose time devoted to childcare averaged 10 hours per week in 1965 and 14 hours per week in 2016. This difference continues to hold as women's average hours at paid work has increased, while that of men have decreased slightly (Livingston and Parker, 2019). Moreover, the Pew data show that perceptions of who is better at childcare reflect a gender bias in favor of mothers; even fathers self-report less confidence in doing childcare than mothers. Thus the time lag between reality and media portrayals of fathers involved in childcare may not apply; screen fathers who are shown participating in the care of their children, or even operating a daycare center (such as in the 2003 comedy film *Daddy Day Care*) might even be ahead of what may be happening in "real life."

Studies of the portrayals of male characters in film and television abound, with gender performative traits associated with hegemonic masculinity observed across media forms. Justification for violence, for example, serves as a recurrent theme in analyses of male characters, as found by Arellano's (2012) study of the cable television series *Dexter* and Scharrer's (2001) content analysis of television police and detective dramas. In addition to applying Trujillo's (1991) summarization of hegemonic masculinity to the character of Anakin Skywalker in the *Star Wars* film franchise, Atkinson and Calafell (2009) argued that Skywalker's use of violence without taking responsibility normalizes such behavior, which in turn "creates spaces of permissiveness for physical violence, sexual violence, harassment and various forms of discrimination" (p. 17). "In the end," they concluded, "the lessons of hegemonic masculinity are taught and naturalized across generations" (p. 17).

Differentiation from femininity serves as a core identifier of Western/U.S. American masculinity, as discussed earlier. Fear of feminization becomes a notable theme that appears to be a conclusion of several studies of male portrayals in films. For example, Hartson (2016) concluded that action hero Jason Bourne, in the *Bourne* franchise of spy thrillers starring Matt Damon that began in 2002, exhibited emotionality, only for that portrayal to be countered by an unemotional efficiency to escape his pursuers: "despite Bourne's apparent paradigm shift toward a kinder, gentler form of masculinity, his behavior on screen remains essentially that of a violent warrior" (p. 51). When one considers the tensions of hegemony, Hartson's observation regarding the Jason Bourne character illustrates how the threat of making Bourne appear almost feminized through his kindly nature is counteracted by reaffirming his competence through violence and the cold dispatching of villains.

Lest such treatments of male-centered texts indicate that tension between the upholding of an idealized masculinity and resistance to that ideal eventually returns it to an abiding, ever-perpetuated form, counterhegemonic versions of masculinity suggest a path for reshaping the mold altogether. The caveat to hegemony theory holds that resistance to dominance both maintains hegemony by presenting instances of difference that uphold normal versus abnormal dichotomies *and* opens the way for counterhegemony that can reach critical mass so as to create a new hegemony. Indeed, one can find examples of portrayals of a "new man," which show characters who embody qualities of masculinity and femininity, are non-conformist, and also interesting and entertaining. These instances drawn from popular entertainment, especially in certain genres that allow for imaginative, unfettered-by-realism narratives and characters, provide nuanced versions of a "new man." This "new man" portrayed on screen could be read as a delayed media representation of what had already existed in the mundane course of everyday life.

Male characters read by scholars as well as online bloggers and commentators (the organic intellectuals Gramsci described) as presenting a "new man" persona in film and television texts include the character of Malcolm Reynolds in the Fox science fiction television series *Firefly* (2002–2003) and subsequent major motion picture *Serenity* (2005). Beadling (2016) traced how the character, created by writer-producer Joss Whedon (known for his strong women characters, such as Buffy the Vampire Slayer), evolved over the course of the short-lived series. Beadling described how Malcolm, a tough war veteran-turned-spaceship captain, exhibited qualities associated with masculine strength as well as a communal mindset indicative of feminine traits. Moreover, Malcolm's treatment of women as individuals and his nonaggressive sexuality (he is celibate in the film and in all but one episode of the series—an episode that did not air, by the way) suggest an egalitarian attitude; this portrayal of the new man "provides a more appealing version of a new masculinity that accepts feminism's ideals without sacrificing toughness or action, essential qualities in the captain of a smuggling vessel" (p. 80). Beadling concluded that this type of character serves as a role model for male viewers in a time when feminism is still treated with hostility, despite the gains of the women's movement.

Asher-Perrin's (2013) unpacking of the character arc of Dean Winchester in the long-running CW horror/fantasy television series *Supernatural* (2005–2020) presents a similar portrait of the new man. Initially fronting a macho exterior (in contrast to his younger brother Sam, who is also strong but the more emotional and sensitive of the two from the start of the series), Dean's inner nerd and emotional expressiveness reveals a man who becomes more comfortable with himself; love for his family and friends serves as an underlying motivation for his actions and his fierce protectiveness of Sam. Dean the "bad boy," argued Asher-Perrin, morphed into man with a "mass of insecurities and hopes," but who eventually becomes unconcerned with performing traits linked to hegemonic masculinity. "He's still gruff, still capable, still tougher than titanium, but no longer feels the need to project socially typified masculine cues to prove himself," noted Asher-Perrin. Like *Firefly*'s Malcolm Reynolds, he serves as a role model for manhood: "Because Dean Winchester proves that there are no boundaries to that definition," she concluded.

A range of masculinities appeared in the NBC comedy *Parks and Recreation* (2009–2015); individual male characters comprising the "new man" persona included the stoic, rugged individualist and egalitarian Ron Swanson; fashion-conscious technophile Tom Haverford; emotionally expressive Chris Traeger; bumbling worker Jerry Girgich; brainy and nerdy Ben Wyatt; and the sweet and silly Andy Dwyer. As the men in the support network of main character and self-professed feminist Leslie Knope, these characters not only offered a range of definitions of manhood, their abiding loyalty and friendship (and, in Ben Wyatt's case, marriage) to her and their treatment of their own romantic partners served as a message of support for feminism in general (Engstrom, 2017). One can consider these "new men"—who incorporate tenets of feminism and egalitarianism—as not only an example of resistance to the stock portrayal of clueless guys typical of network comedy, but also as positive models for the advancement of entertainment that also communicates the message that men are and can be feminists.

The Andy Dwyer character's television alter ego known as "Johnny Karate" adds another facet to the portrayal of men in the series, in that the verbalization and promotion of feminine-typed traits is brought to the fore. As the host of a children's television show, Johnny Karate espouses and teaches the children who make up his audience (and, by proxy, the viewers of *Parks and Recreation*) to be kind and honest. His kids' TV show also demonstrates the importance of expressing affection with a segment called "Hug

Moment." The "five karate" moves to success espoused in the Johnny Karate philosophy include the following directives, with traits emphasized in parentheses: learn something new (intellectual curiosity), try something new (self-development and growth mindset), make something (creativity), karate chop something (physical fitness), and the most important step to success, be kind to someone (kindness, yes, but also thoughtfulness and sensitivity). Although the moves are mentioned in just one episode of the series, their very inclusion in a primetime television series illustrates Gramsci's maxim that media of merit contain moral content. The success of *Parks and Recreation*, whose excellence was marked by critical acclaim and awards, serves as an example of the blending of prosocial messaging with entertaining, clever creativity in a capitalistic media environment.[4]

The Pixar universe of computer-animated films, such as the *Toy Story*, *The Incredibles*, and *Cars* franchises, offers an amalgam of male protagonists whose character arcs led to a "new man" persona that similarly embodies feminine-typed traits. Gillam and Wooden (2008) called this "Pixar's new man," whereby alpha-male types face tests of character such as failure and humiliation that result in their self-realization that prototypical masculinity does not work for them any longer: they must reject norms of masculinity in order to achieve group goals, and thereby take on behaviors that push against their own self-image. Notable among the traits Gillam and Wooden point out these male characters exhibit through the course of their personal growth are emotional expressivity, giving and receiving care, communal cooperation, empathy, and dependence on others. As avatars (literally) for real-life men and boys, these examples from a group of mainly light-hearted family films offer the possibility for media to depict a revised masculinity more in tune with a gender-progressive mindset. Pixar's new men (whether depicted as toys, humans with superpowers, or cars) "achieve and (and teach) a kinder, gentler understanding of what it means to be a man," argued Gillam and Wooden (p. 3).

In a follow-up book expanding their investigation into the implications of Pixar's media offerings regarding contemporary boyhood, Wooden and Gillam (2014) described Pixar's films as offering "a breath of fresh air" for parents of boys; "the films that have come out of Pixar seem to tell a very different story of masculinity than that promoted by Disney's other products," such as the films of the Marvel Cinematic Universe, the franchise of films based on the superheroes of Marvel Comics (p. xxiv). Even though Pixar's new man may suggest that cultural products created solely for entertainment and profit can serve as sources for alternate ways of portraying gender, the need to critically approach them remains. Lest the beloved status of Disney and the aura of its imprimatur distract audiences from reflecting on the gendered messages of seemingly innocent stories of talking cars and toys that come to life, Wooden and Gillam warn that "as parents and critics, we need to pay close attention. As much as anything we do or say, these cultural pedagogies are teaching our boys what it means to be men" (p. 142). Although the (men) superheroes of the Marvel Cinematic Universe (MCU) that Wooden and Gillam mentioned may present obvious and expected versions of masculinity that appear as common sense—what else could superheroes be but strong, confident, self-reliant, and super manly?—a media literacy approach informed by the theory of hegemonic masculinity and its companionate implications provides a path of inquiry that we see as a means to illustrate Gramscian hegemony in action.

MEDIATED MASCULINITY AND THE MCU

The superhero genre of storytelling, originating from U.S. comic books dating from the late 1930s, centers on morality tales featuring characters with superhuman powers, usually distinguished by a special costume or physical appearance, codename, and at times a "regular" human alter ego (Reinhard & Olson, 2018). Characters' origin stories and narrative tropes concerning conflict of some kind serve as common threads within the genre. "Regardless of the story being told, or how it was told, the characters provided the main defining parameters for the genre, and their conflicts became the means by which creators and audiences could address problems in the real world," according to Reinhard and Olson (2018, p. 4).

Gender representation of superhero texts readily lends itself to critical analysis. For example, Roublou (2009) invoked Connell's aforementioned concept of hegemonic masculinity to examine how the appearance of male superheroes perpetuates gender difference by amplifying the muscularity associated with idealized masculinity. Noting that superheroes originally appeared in their comic book iteration as "hyperbolically masculine," Roublou pointed out that male superheroes rarely openly question their own masculinity, but may question the masculinity of their enemies. As unrealistic and fantastical as they are, superhero texts add to a continuum of media artifacts and the "reproduction—and hence the continuity—of cultural fictions concerning masculinity" (p. 77).

In a book-length treatment of the Marvel Cinematic Universe, McSweeney (2018) took a Gramscian approach to his analyses of MCU films, arguing that even if some might consider popular films and television texts "frivolities" (p. 15), to study them is to tap into the pervading cultural ideology of the time, which contributes to hegemonic systems of power. Further, popular media don't just reflect cultural discourse but also contribute to it. For McSweeney, the MCU "provides us with a range of affective texts which function as an embodiment of their era in a range of ways," with those texts serving as ideological discourse in materialized form (p. 16). Explicitly American-coded discourse imbued in the MCU revolves around the wish-fulfillment of fantasies at two levels: the desire to be "stronger, faster, more virile, and more attractive" at the individual level, and empowerment on the world stage at the national level, argued McSweeney (p. 19).

Regarding the men of the MCU, they similarly represent not only the "American hero" persona but also its cultural values. Citing Roublou's (2009) essay on the overly muscular superhero body, McSweeney also addressed the MCU's portrayal of superhero bodies as symbolizing national (American) identity. However, masculinity itself within the MCU, as "literalised" by individual superheroes who do not all follow the same pattern of physical appearance or performance of masculinity, "can be seen to display a more unstable and variegated depiction of masculinity, although no less hegemonic" (p. 26). This variegation, as we will address in the following chapter, extends beyond the wide range of character personalities, the symbolism of their codename and mission, and body types to the expanding of the definition of masculinity to one more reflective of changing notions of gender.

In unpacking the hugely successful 2012 MCU ensemble film *The Avengers*, which brought the Marvel superheroes together, McGrath (2016) noted that the Avengers team of superheroes "demonstrated a model of heterosocial collaborative masculinity that contrasts against the hyper-masculine that is traditionally associated with other superhero stories" (p. 136). Building on previous MCU offerings, McGrath explained that *The Avengers* provided "representations of post-feminist masculinity as multivalent rather than one-dimensional" (p. 135). In contrast to the front of confidence and self-reliance typically associated with masculinity, as discussed earlier in this chapter, McGrath argued that the male Avengers "appear as more flawed, subject to bouts of self-doubt and assuming roles as nurturers to their peers regardless of gender," while the female superheroes tended toward more masculine-typed behaviors (p. 138). Regarding the visual presentation of characters onscreen, however, female superheroes were still subjected to the male gaze historical of Hollywood films, with their costuming calling attention to their bodies. This aspect of gendered cultural production even appeared to apply to the male superheroes, noted McGrath, with the male characters' toned arms and physiques on display.

McGrath addressed the nuance in the masculinity portrayals of particular male superheroes, such as Iron Man/Tony Stark, Captain America/Steve Rogers, and Hawkeye/Clint Barton. For example, Tony Stark, who previously resisted emotional closeness with and dependence on others, undergoes a transformation that sees him engaging in teamwork and collaboration, similar to the way Pixar's new man learns the value of communal effort. Clint Barton, the team's happily married family man, devoted to his wife and children, displays parental and motherly qualities—a kind of role reversal vis-à-vis his work partnership with Black Widow/Natasha Romanova. Notably, it is Captain America/Steve Rogers, whom one can read as the superhero reification of "America" writ large, that McGrath described as an example of a "new masculinity" that combines culturally defined traits associated with both masculinity and femininity. Rogers—whose origin story is that of a World War II American soldier—"retains a pure innocence actually suited to 21st century understandings of 'new masculinity,'" observed McGrath (2016, p. 140). McGrath's queer reading of the Tony Stark-Steve Rogers relationship, marked by antagonism and verbal sparring, described it as "teeming with sexual subtext" that points to both characters' "metrosexual" qualities (p. 141). The way in which this homosocial partnership between two men who may appear as opposites (the cynical, sarcastic Stark and the "square" and innocent all-American Rogers) adds another facet to the reshaping of masculinity reflected in *The Avengers*, which was written and directed by Joss Whedon, a cultural producer known for attending to and challenging the gender status quo. *The Avengers* was followed by three more ensemble offerings: *Avengers: Age of Ultron* (2015), *Avengers: Infinity War* (2018), and the denouement *Avengers: Endgame* (2019). The Tony Stark-Steve Rogers bantering continues in *Avengers: Endgame*, with additional nuance that furthers a characterization of masculinity that suggests psychological intimacy as a facet of male-male friendships as we describe in the next chapter.

CONCLUSION AND PREVIEW

We have argued here that among status quo versions of manhood that still permeate the contemporary mass media landscape, there do exist oppositional portrayals of men that reject outright the hegemonic masculinity that has become common sense. The "new men" we have described in this chapter meld the best of what are still considered manly traits (strength, independence) with those considered "feminine" (communal effort, nurturing, emotional expressivity) to create androgynous and more complete versions of human beings. In that strictly adhering to the "man rules" limits human potential and manifests in limited emotional expressivity and other unhealthy results, as described by Levant (2011), when media perpetuate gender stereotypes to the point where they seem "normal," those instances in which we see male characters *not* being "macho" become even more noticeable. Hence, when counterhegemony appears, it may either threaten the status quo

or create a new path for exploring the possibilities of a new way of thinking, creating, and even enjoying those media that dare to take us down that
unexplored road.

In the following chapter, we examine the portrayal of male lead characters
in the 2019 Marvel/Disney film *Avengers: Endgame* (hereafter referred to as
Endgame), which served as the denouement of a franchise of twenty-three
filmic versions of Marvel's comic books spanning the course of twelve
years. Indeed, the financial success of the MCU redefined film franchise
history (Harrison et al., 2019). Together these films amassed some $22 bil-
lion in ticket sales worldwide, emphasizing the "popular" in popular culture
(Bean, 2020). In 2019, ticket sales for *Endgame*, a 3-hour and 1-minute cinematic epic, totaled more than $858 million dollars in the United States, and
almost $2 billion internationally, with close to $3 billion overall (*Avengers:
Endgame*, n.d.). Released in April 2019, by July it had become the highest-
grossing film of all time (Whitten, 2019).

We approach the film's various portrayals of its male superheroes through
the lens of hegemonic masculinity, which relies on Gramsci's theory of
hegemony as a foundation for explaining gender difference and the hierarchies of privilege between genders and within them as well. In that
hegemonic struggle requires a push-pull dynamic between the status quo
and social change, our exploration of what we call "Marvel's New Man"
also must consider the continuum of gender difference, if any, whereupon
this version of manliness may lie. Given that in the MCU both males and
females (human, alien, and otherwise) are depicted as having extraordinary
powers and abilities, in that sense one could consider it an egalitarian social
structure. However, in that Western/U.S. culture in particular is still imbued
with socially constructed schema regarding what is considered masculine
and feminine, or, on occasion both (androgyny), the exploration of gender
portrayal as a manifestation of hegemonic struggle becomes even more
relevant.

Although our focus centers on portrayals of male superheroes in the last
of the MCU's financial and overall critical success, our discussion also must
address how these portrayals function against the obvious comparison to
how women superheroes are portrayed. Thus, in the next chapter, we deconstruct how MCU superhero characters, such as Tony Stark/Iron Man, Steve
Rogers/Captain America, Bruce Banner/The Hulk, and Thor, are portrayed
through a gendered lens. Following our analysis of how their composite
portrayals in *Endgame* push the boundaries of hegemonic masculinity to
encroach upon gender-fluid territory, we consider our observations within
the context of how these instances of on-the-surface change in how men are
presented to viewers compare to portrayals of women superheroes in the
same text.

NOTES

1. For more on how Gramsci and hegemony relate directly to gender, and women's and feminist studies, in particular, see Arnot (1982), Buttigieg (2002), Dombroski (1986), Garcia (1992), Holub (1992), Landy (1986), Lather (1984), Ledwith (2009), and Sassoon (1987).

2. Conceptualized by Australian sociologist Raewyn Connell (who had published under the name R.W. Connell prior to 2005) in the 1980s, hegemonic masculinity explains how gender inequality becomes legitimate and maintains differentiation not only in the status between masculinity and femininity but also in the hierarchies between masculinities; in Western culture, the highest status and privilege tends to be accorded to White, heterosexual masculinity (Messerschmidt, 2018).

3. See Levant (2011) for more on traditional masculinity norms, normative male alexithymia, and the negative personal and societal consequences of strict gender socialization of boys. Levant synthesizes his and other research on the psychology of men that ties cultural norms to the reasons for why the study of men and boys is vital to not only understanding how hegemonic notions of gender function and affect everyone, but how to achieve gender equality.

4. See Yahr (2015), who explained the reasons for the show's critical praise. In 2011, the show won a Peabody Award; *Parks and Recreation* co-creator Michael Schur cited hard work, citizenship and public service, and kindness as virtues celebrated by the show (*Parks and Recreation*, NBC, 2011).

Chapter 5

The Gendered *Endgame*

Marvel's New Man

Avengers: Endgame opens with Clint Barton/Hawkeye teaching his daughter archery; his family is having a picnic at his farm. He turns for a second and his whole family has disappeared. This alludes to "the Snap," when half of all life on Earth and in the universe vanished at the end of *Avengers: Infinity War*. *Endgame* follows the Avengers after their humiliating, soul-crushing defeat at the hands, literally, of Thanos, the all-powerful being whose mission was to bring balance back to the universe by eliminating half of all life. Thanos wore a gauntlet containing the Infinity Stones—stones with magical properties—and snapped his fingers at the end of *Infinity War* to make half of all living creatures in the universe disappear, including several superheroes. In the days after the Snap, Tony Stark/Iron Man is close to death, and being nursed by Nebula, Thanos's adopted daughter, on a dead-in-space vessel. Just when it seems all is lost and Tony may die, Carol Danvers/Captain Marvel finds them and takes them to the Avengers' headquarters on Earth. After Tony reunites with the Avengers, Nebula helps the team find Thanos on a distant planet in order to retrieve the gauntlet and snap the lives lost back into existence. But when they arrive, Thanos tells them he had already used the gauntlet to make it and the stones disappear. Thor, in a fit of rage, chops Thanos's head off. It seems the Avengers have no recourse to make the universe right again. They are defeated—again—with no hope of bringing back their loved ones and all who were lost because of Thanos's actions.

The story moves ahead five years. By this time, Tony Stark has left the Avengers life; he married his longtime girlfriend Pepper Potts and they have a young daughter named Morgan. Steve Rogers/Captain America runs a support group for survivors of the Snap, and Natasha Romanova/Black Widow has become the Avengers' leader, running operations from the Avengers' headquarters. Bruce Banner/Hulk has figured out a way to meld his Hulk and

Banner identities; he is referred to in the film's subtitles as "Smart Hulk." Thor has retreated to New Asgard, a community of remaining Asgardians. He spends his days getting drunk, eating junk food, and playing video games.

Scott Lang/Ant-Man has reemerged from the quantum realm he was stuck in when the Snap occurred, and finds his way to Avengers headquarters. He convinces Natasha and Steve that they could travel through the quantum realm and through time to retrieve the Infinity Stones in order to snap the universe back to normal and bring back all the people who were lost. Natasha, Steve, and Scott visit Tony at his home retreat in the country, and try to convince him that time travel could work, but he rejects the idea, not wanting to risk losing his family if the plan went wrong. Eventually, he shows up at Avengers headquarters after discovering time travel could work. The team devises a plan to travel back in time to take the Infinity Stones, which exist at different locations at different times. They work in pairs and small groups, with their efforts to obtain the stones diverging into separate narratives. In the one that has Tony and Steve finding a stone in 1970, Tony (disguised as a scientist) meets his father just prior to his own birth.

Eventually, the Avengers are successful in getting all the Stones, but not before losing Natasha, who sacrifices herself in order to retrieve the "Soul Stone" during her and Clint's mission. The stone required the sacrifice of a life in order to be retrieved. Both Natasha and Clint think they are going to be that sacrifice, but Natasha outsmarts Clint as they are struggling against each other on the side of a cliff, and plunges to her death. Her loss is grieved by the remaining Avengers, who are determined to continue their quest to avenge her death.

As the Avengers are recovering the stones, Thanos learns of their plan, and with the help of a past, crueler version of Nebula, finds his way back to Earth in order to prevent them from completing their mission. Thanos does not arrive until after Hulk uses a gauntlet made by Tony to hold the Infinity Stones and snaps back all the lives lost five years earlier. Just as it seemed the team's plan had worked, Thanos appears with a massive army of aliens, and begins an epic battle at which all the missing Avengers allies—including Peter Parker/Spider-Man, Wanda Maximoff/Scarlet Witch, T'Challa/Black Panther, and Steven Strange/Dr. Strange—reappear. The battle evokes imagery of World War II's D-Day invasion on a planetary scale, with all the Marvel superheroes, except Natasha, fighting the forces of Thanos. Thanos manages to get the new gauntlet, even after being held by Captain Marvel/Carol Danvers, whose powers equal that of Thanos. The stones are finally obtained by Tony Stark, who uses them to snap Thanos out of existence, but not before their immense gamma-ray energy mortally wounds him.

Following Tony's memorial service, attended by various Avengers and other key Marvel characters, Hulk sends Steve back in time to put the Infinity

Stones in their original timelines. Steve returns from this last time-travel mission in just minutes, but is now an old man. He hands over his iconic shield to Sam Wilson/Falcon, in essence making Sam the new Captain America. The film concludes with a scene of Steve in his younger form dancing with his true love, Peggy Carter, indicating he stayed back in time to live the life that had essentially been taken from him when he was transformed into Captain America during World War II. The film ends the Avengers franchise with credits showing all the Marvel superheroes. The final character that appears in the closing sequence featuring each of the principal Avengers is Tony Stark/Iron Man, which serves as a salute to the first of the MCU films, 2008's *Iron Man*.

HEGEMONIC MASCULINITY AND MARVEL'S NEW MAN

Blumberg (2014) argued the merits of using popular culture and the MCU in particular to teach critical thinking, and to spark such thinking about social issues like gender, race, class, and morality. This approach reflects Gramsci's edict that cultural products contain moral content. "The superhero genre also offers insights into human relationships and transcendent mysteries of hope, friendship, goodness and love that bind people together and give them purpose," argued Hodge (2018). Acu (2016) framed the composite narrative of the Avengers as a workplace story that emphasizes teamwork, noting that the MCU changed the superhero genre from a theme of "the ability to do anything to the ability to meaningfully contribute through one's affiliation" (p. 197). Regarding *Endgame* specifically, Debruge (2019) commented on the film's themes of personal sacrifice, heroism, and the importance of family. Gideonse (2019) similarly highlighted the theme of heroism, adding how the film "resonates if not universally then damn near close."

Writing about the MCU for the online film criticism website */Film*, Jones (2017) noted: "Whether you realize it or not, it's considered one of the biggest pop culture institutions defining modern American manhood." With its multiple narratives centering on the male superheroes in particular, the MCU invites a textual analysis of specific interactions and dialogue illustrative of the struggle between status quo maintenance and its companionate resistance implicit in the concept of hegemonic masculinity. Regarding *Endgame* specifically, critics and commentators noted its positive portrayals of masculinity (Anthony, 2019; Brusuelas, 2019; Carlson, 2020; Rojas, 2019), as well as its problematic treatment of specific characters that appeared to perpetuate ideals of traditional masculinity (Brusuelas, 2019; Dana, 2019; Mohan, 2019; Rojas, 2019; White, 2019).

Relying on hegemonic masculinity as a theoretical foundation, the concept of normative male alexithymia, and studies that have identified characteristics of "the new man" as depicted across media forms discussed in the previous chapter, we examine *Endgame* using a close reading of the film's dialogue, imagery, character interactions, and overall portrayals of characters to identify the components of Marvel's new man that offer a counterhegemonic masculinity. Five themes emerged from this reading: seeking help from and giving help to others, emotional expressiveness, expressions of fear and vulnerability, and emphasis on father–child relationships.

MARVEL'S NEW MAN ASKS FOR AND GIVES HELP

Throughout *Endgame*, several male Avengers and superheroes offer counterhegemonic portrayals that reject the masculine traits of self-reliance and avoidance of appearing weak and seeking help from others. Several scenes throughout the film illustrate the giving of help to and requests for help from others by the male superheroes, in contrast to the traditional masculine trope of independence, which promotes a self-identity of being independent and perceiving others as independent enough not to require help. The giving of help as a trait of Marvel's new man is exemplified by Steve Rogers's involvement with a post-Snap support group. In an early scene in the film that depicts life five years after half of the world's living creatures are gone, the viewer gets a sweeping view over New York City, which appears gray and depressing, a deteriorating city. Steve is shown leading a support group for survivors. The group listens to a man describing how he finally asked someone for a date, and that he and his date cried during their dinner. "I'm seeing him again," the man concludes, to which Steve replies, calmly and encouragingly, "That's great. You did the hardest part. You took the jump. You didn't know where you were gonna come down. And that's it. That's those little brave baby steps we gotta take to try and become whole again, try to find purpose."[1] Steve then reveals to the group his own personal history and how he found a way to move on after heartache, alluding to his lost love, Peggy Carter. "I went into the ice in '45, right after I met the love of my life. Woke up 70 years later. You gotta move on. Gotta move on," he says.

Not only is Steve's involvement with the support group a demonstration of his personal mission to help others, but it also normalizes support groups and the seeking of help as a way to cope with emotional problems and trauma.[2] Carlson (2020) addressed Steve's involvement with the support group as showing how this muscular superhero struggles emotionally, describing the scene at the support group meeting as "a moment of quiet reflection that isn't found in superhero movies." This becomes more notable in that it is Steve, a man, leading a support group, and the scene features another man talking about being emotionally expressive. Steve's own self-disclosure further illustrates a characteristic of the feminine style of communication, which features an egalitarian stance when communicating with others (Fixmer-Oraiz and Wood, 2019). The "me, too" approach creates a sense of equality between interactants; this is shown through one's self-disclosure and including others within one's ego boundary, the psychological dividing line between the self and the rest of the world. In a sense, Steve is saying that he is one of the group, rather than the "leader" who knows more than they do. When he says, "You gotta move on," he isn't just talking to the group, but the viewer gets the sense that he is also advising himself to move on and find a way forward.

Regarding Steve's ability to nurture, Rojas (2019) pointed to the way he interacts with Natasha when he visits her at Avengers headquarters in a sequence that comes after the support group scene. The two talk about how they're coping, and the prospect of moving past the trauma of the Snap and their failed attempt at getting the Infinity Stones from Thanos five years earlier. In that Steve doesn't tell her what to do about her grief, Rojas noted, he "is able to be present with her." In this manner, "Steve demonstrates what masculinity looks like when empathy is the driving force behind it," Rojas concluded.

Verbalizing that one needs help adds to this aspect of a new version of masculinity as portrayed in *Endgame*. In the epic battle with Thanos toward the end of the film, in which the superheroes are in the fight of their lives, the returned Peter Parker/Spider-Man has the Infinity Stone gauntlet and tries to take it across the battlefield to Ant-Man's time machine, a dilapidated brown van. Alien creatures from Thanos's army surround Peter and overrun him. He says aloud to himself, "I got this. I got this." Realizing he is in trouble, he then admits, "Okay. I don't got this." He shouts, "Help! Somebody help!" Steve Rogers hears him, and sends Thor's hammer to pull him up from the melee. As Peter spins a web around the flying hammer, the web is shot by incoming fire. Pepper Potts, in her Iron Woman armored suit, rescues him. "Hang on, kid, I gotcha," she says. Then she hands him over to Valkyrie, another female superhero. Peter's explicit cry for help demonstrates the willingness and realization by a male character—a superhero, no less—that he needs help. His rescue by two women further shows that help can come from anyone willing and able, not only another male.

The battle scene in *Endgame* includes another request for help by a man to a woman. When Carol Danvers/Captain Marvel arrives from outer space midway through the battle between Thanos and the superheroes, she is immediately called upon by Steve. After Pepper Potts and then Valkyrie rescue Peter Parker, he still needs help to get the gauntlet across the battlefield. Steve then calls on Carol to help: "Danvers, we need an assist," he tells her.

Steve's verbalization to Carol—a sort of bookend to how he was offering help at the support group at the beginning of the film—not only reaffirms the importance of teamwork over a focus on the individual but echoes the earlier call for help by Peter, showing that Marvel's new man is not concerned about looking weak when asking for and getting help. Further, showing that help is given when asked emphasizes that relying on others when one is in need or in trouble can lead to a successful outcome.

MARVEL'S NEW MAN IS EMOTIONALLY EXPRESSIVE

Throughout *Endgame*, demonstrations of emotion are a common occurrence among and between the male superheroes. This expression includes both nonverbal and verbal communication of a range of feelings, including gratitude, trust, love, sadness, grief, and admiration. These superheroes visibly cry, such as when Thor sees his mother when he time travels to Asgard, when Peter tells Tony they won the battle at the end of the film while Tony is dying, and when Rhodey/War Machine is with Tony's family to view Tony's recorded message he made before rejoining the Avengers to embark on their mission. Hawkeye's look of grief and anguish when Natasha sacrifices herself to obtain the Soul Stone illustrates how un-stoic these men are, in contrast to how boys and men are socialized to be emotionally reserved.

Tony Stark, in particular, is portrayed in several scenes as freely expressing nonverbal signs of affection through the nonverbal tie-sign of the embrace. During his and Steve's mission to correct their failure to retrieve one of the stones (in the form of the Tesseract), they go back further in time to 1970 when it was at a New Jersey army base. Tony's father, Howard Stark, happens to be there right when they arrive. Tony, disguised as a scientist, encounters him. Though Tony is older than his father in this scene, when Howard asks him for advice on becoming a father to his soon-to-be-born baby (Tony), Tony obliges. Clearly feeling somewhat overwhelmed at meeting his own father before he was even born, Tony nevertheless reassures his father, ironically by talking about what kind of father Howard was to him. "I thought my dad was tough on me," he admits to Howard. "And now, looking back on it, I just remember the good stuff, you know?" They continue talking, with Howard admitting to Tony: "I'll tell you, that kid's not even here yet and there's nothing I wouldn't do for him." They shake hands as Howard takes his leave. Tony then moves to embrace his father and says, "Thank you for everything," he says, then catches himself, realizing that he's just a stranger to his father, ". . . you've done for this country." He embraces a man he supposedly just met, reflecting his love for his father and his ability to express his feelings through this nonverbal sign of connection.

Tony's emotional expressiveness is shown again in the scene in which he is reunited with Peter Parker in the battle sequence toward the end of the film. Tony does not hesitate to show his affection for his young protégé, who he thought was gone forever after the Snap. As Peter breathlessly explains to Tony how it was he arrived at the battlefield just moments prior, Tony does not say a word but quickly hugs him instead. "What are you doing?" asks Peter, confused at Tony's embrace. Understanding that Tony is showing him affection, Peter then utters, "Oh." Relaxing in the embrace, Peter adds, "This is nice." This sweet yet comical scene reflects a deep attachment between Tony and Peter, demonstrating that real men do hug each other, and can verbalize their appreciation for such a moment. Culturally speaking, U.S. touch norms dictate little public touch between men, so this and other times when the male superheroes embrace each other counter the expectation that men avoid nonverbal expressions of attachment (Knapp and Hall, 2009). Peter's comment that it was nice further alludes to the benefits of human touch, as it provides what famed researcher Harry Harlow termed "contact comfort" (American Psychological Association, 2020).

Expressions of caring and attachment are demonstrated by Thor, who, as described later, easily shows emotions and verbalizes his feelings. When he and Rocket Raccoon are in 2013 Asgard, Thor's home, he encounters his mother, Frigga. Realizing that on that very day in 2013 she will die, he starts getting weepy. Thor's depressive state since he killed Thanos five years earlier has manifested in his overeating, overdrinking, and generally being a sloppy mess. Frigga knows he is from the future. He discloses to her how he thinks he has become a failure; she explains to him that perhaps he is, but that no one becomes who they are supposed to be. As they part ways, she tells him, "Now you go and be the man you're *meant* to be." As he and Rocket leave, Thor says, "I love you, Mom." Frigga replies, "I love you." They hug, and then she adds, "And eat a salad." This last comment about his weight may appear humorous, but can be read also as either a mother showing concern about her child's health or the writers making light of a serious problem. Either way, Thor's verbalizing to his mother that he loves her illustrates a rejection of normative male alexithymia, and thus the tenet of hegemonic masculinity that men restrain from showing emotion.

Verbalization of admiration characterizes in particular Scott Lang/Ant-Man's "man crush" on Steve Rogers/Captain America. In several scenes, Scott openly expresses his high regard for Steve. When Hulk, Natasha, and Steve conduct time-travel experiments using Scott as the "guinea pig," Steve reassures Scott, "You got this." Scott smiles at Steve with genuine affection and replies, "You're right. I do, Captain America." When the team finally embarks on their mission to get the Infinity Stones after Tony Stark figures out how to correctly time travel, they are gathered together to make the jump into the quantum realm. Steve gives a pep talk—in his inimitable and serious way—telling the team, "We have a plan: six stones, three teams, one shot. Be careful. Look out for each other. This is the fight of our lives. And we're gonna win. Whatever it takes." As Steve speaks, Tony looks at him with a slight smile, a facial expression that appears to show appreciation for Steve's inspirational speech. Rocket then declares to the others, "He's pretty good at that." Scott smiles enthusiastically, and replies in agreement, "Right?"

Scott's admiration for Steve becomes even more significant in a scene that not only illustrates open communication between men but also puts a twist on the male gaze, which historically concerns the way women are physically presented through the lens of a male director and male viewer. When he, Steve, Tony, and Hulk arrive in 2012 New York to retrieve one of the stones, they are at Stark Industries headquarters, watching their 2012 selves. When Tony sees 2012 Steve/Captain America, he makes a comment about his appearance. With Scott miniaturized as Ant-Man standing on Tony's shoulder, Tony says to Steve with a scoff, "Mr. Rogers, I almost forgot. That suit did nothing for your ass." Steve hears Tony's remark in his earpiece and replies, "No one asked you to look, Tony." "It's ridiculous," Tony further comments. This commentary by Tony about Steve's body and Steve's nonchalant retort allows for two men coded as straight to not only acknowledge that a man can "check out" another man without fear of offense, but it adds humor and comic relief to their once-strained relationship. When Scott joins their back-and-forth banter to defend Steve from Tony's assessment, his open admiration for Steve becomes even more notable. "I think you look great, Cap," Scott declares. "As far as I'm concerned, that's America's ass," he says confidently, saluting while he gives this compliment to Steve. This subversion of the male gaze has men scrutinizing each other with ease and even humor, which violates the homophilic tension theorized by Laura Mulvey's (1975) now-classic explanation of the male gaze as a gendered practice that keeps patriarchy emplaced by making women the objects of the gaze, rather than the subject doing the gazing. By having Tony and Scott focusing their gaze on Steve, it ruptures hegemonic patriarchy—which in turn becomes a way to remold hegemonic masculinity.

The male gaze becomes even further subverted when Steve encounters his 2012 self a few minutes later. 2012 Captain America thinks his 2023 version is actually the Avengers' nemesis Loki, the brother of Thor, in disguise. The two Captains fight each other, and 2023 Captain finally defeats his 2012 self, causing him to become unconscious. As his 2012 self lies on the floor face down, Steve looks at his own backside, and confirms Scott's earlier conclusion by saying, "That *is* America's ass." Here, Steve gazes at himself, which inverts the male gaze to the point that it is self-gaze. One can read this as a humorous turn, but it points to how *Endgame*'s writers manage to present a body positivity for men that plays on the often negative way that women self-criticize their own physical appearance. Taken further, one can argue that this serves as a commentary on how patriarchy keeps women from empowering themselves because of the constant surveillance they experience in a society that overvalues women for their appearance. Rather than worry about their bodies, women instead should take a cue from Steve Rogers.

MARVEL'S NEW MAN SHOWS FEAR AND VULNERABILITY

Expressions of fear and doubt permeate the portrayals of the male superheroes throughout the film. These include admitting not having confidence, such as when Scott Lang/Ant-Man admits that he wasn't prepared for the time-travel experiments, and Peter Parker/Spider-Man realizes he is in trouble during the battle scene and has to cry out for help. Tony Stark's self-disclosing of doubts and misgivings becomes part of his character arc; the once-arrogant industrialist tells Steve Rogers that he cannot risk losing his wife and daughter should the time-travel mission go wrong. When he arrives at Avengers headquarters after he discovers how to make time travel work correctly, he tells Steve: "We got a shot at getting these stones, but I gotta tell you my priorities. Bring back what we've lost. I hope, yes. Keep what I found. I have to, at all costs. And, maybe not die trying would be nice." Tony's explanation hints that he was conflicted about rejoining the Avengers, and his self-disclosure illustrates a fear of losing his family in pursuit of their mission to save the universe.

Of the Avengers men who most prominently express fear and vulnerability, the once-mighty and fearless Thor openly communicates self-doubt the most. Still coping with loss and defeat, and his own killing of Thanos that seemed to end any hope that they could bring back all the lost lives taken in the Snap, he has become mired in a state of depression. Physically and emotionally, Thor appears as if he has given up. When Hulk and Rocket visit him at New Asgard to persuade him to rejoin the team, he starts getting weepy at the mention of Thanos. Only through Hulk's gentle tone and expression of caring does Thor seem to calm down. Later, when he and Rocket are in 2013 Asgard, the sight of his mother emotionally overwhelms him. "I think I'm having a panic attack," he admits to Rocket. "I can't do this. I can't do this," he repeats frantically. Rocket's response is to disclose that he, too, is suffering from the loss of the only family he ever knew. He explains that Thor can't bring his mother back, but can help get back those who were lost in the Snap. "Okay," says Thor, who starts crying again. "Are you crying?" asks Rocket, to which Thor says no, then yes. "I think I'm losing it," Thor says, panicking and hyperventilating. Rocket again reassures Thor that he can go through with the mission, but when Rocket's back is turned, Thor makes a run for it. Only when his mother finds him and after talking with his mother and she encourages him does Thor regain his composure. Thor even tells her, "I need to talk to you." This utterance underscores the importance of putting one's emotions and feelings into words—the very opposite of normative male alexithymia. Thor's need to talk to his mother and unburden his anxiety to her further shows the importance of talking out one's troubles rather than tamping down one's anxiety in order to keep up a front that belies internal emotional turmoil.

In *Endgame*, men's ability to admit fear and self-doubt becomes normalized—and their at-times lack of self-confidence exposes them as humans with feelings and, perhaps more importantly in the context of normative male alexithymia, their ability to openly *express* those feelings. Combined with the expression of affection and attachment, these verbalizations of fear and vulnerability dismantle hegemonic masculinity and its mandate that real men "suck it up" and keep their feelings hidden. Further, these mediated depictions of (albeit fictional) men communicate to audiences that truly strong men can show that they are weak. "Vulnerability can be heroic," noted Anthony (2019), in a positive review of the film. Indeed, the Avengers films that comprise the Infinity Saga, of which *Endgame* serves as the conclusion, offer not just entertainment and profit but also models for validating more expansive versions of masculinity. This group of films, concluded Anthony, "highlights the flaws and virtues of being a man in a surprisingly illuminating and moving way. It encouragingly shows their willingness to change and either move past those flaws or embrace them to better understand who they are and those they care about."

Not only do these myriad depictions in the film offer a counterhegemonic version of heroic, "manly" men, but traditional notions of masculine behavior become further dismantled when considering that these traits not only are still coded as feminine but also can be read as feminist. Brusuelas (2019) connected the emotional experiences encouraged by *Endgame*'s male protagonists to the feminist foundation of egalitarianism; the front of hegemonic masculinity obscures gender equality by creating a false difference based on the irrational idea that men shouldn't show their humanness. "Addressing our emotions—failure, guilt, sadness, emptiness—all of this is innately feminist because it allows us to really see the human nature of these characters instead of what we want them to be," Brusuelas asserted.

This is not to say *Endgame*'s portrayal of a character like Thor has no problems. Thor clearly could benefit from a support group like the one Steve leads. There is still quite a bit of room for improvement, such as not making light of his obvious need for therapy. A man crying shouldn't be funny, and rather than have Rocket slap him and tell him to essentially "snap out of it" and get to work, a serious response (and one that would model how Thor's anxiety should be addressed) would have Thor seeking real help (Brusuelas, 2019; Dana, 2019; Rojas, 2019). Rojas (2019) also offers a positive reading, noting how Thor "steps into battle alongside his team, demonstrating that body size, trauma, and depression do not make a man any less worthy," an assessment similar to Anthony's (2019) regarding how this male superhero overcomes despair to join his friends in their fight to save the universe. Although Hulk does show compassion and concern for Thor, the inclusion of a serious treatment of Thor's dilemma that shows the benefits of getting help would have moved the film more in the direction of its already prosocial *gestalt*. Even with this shortcoming, however, *Endgame* addresses and corrects a criticism made by Jones (2017) about previous MCU offerings. Jones argued for depictions of men superheroes that show more than just "anger and snarkiness," and for men to be allowed to cry and still be seen as strong. In *Endgame* they do, and in so doing deconstruct hegemonic masculinity and its negative implications.

MARVEL'S NEW MAN PRIORITIZES HIS FAMILY (AND DOES CHILDCARE)

Although *Endgame* is an action movie in the superhero genre, as a text it reads more like a conventional human drama, one that revolves around surmounting obstacles faced by "regular" humans in everyday life. It is a story of a group of individuals who face a big problem they must overcome, and each of them deals with solving that problem in addition to dealing with personal issues. Threading through the overall storyline and each character's narrative is the theme of family, whether biological or defined by the close personal ties between the Avengers themselves. Indeed, the opening scene of *Endgame* centers on family when Clint Barton teaches archery, his expert skill, to his daughter Lila. Clint already had left the Avengers, seeking a quiet life with his family on their farm earlier in the Avengers saga. His devotion to his family, and his decision to give up the Avengers life in favor of a quiet life with his family, counters the traditionally masculine priority of being the breadwinner (Fixmer-Oraiz & Wood, 2019).

As undramatic as Clint's home life appears, his storyline adds to a portrayal of masculinity that emphasizes the male parental role, especially regarding fathers and daughters. The scene depicts the family getting ready for an outdoor picnic, its time setting the very moment of the Snap that occurred at the end of Infinity War. Clint turns his attention away from his daughter for a split second, and suddenly his family has disappeared. This symbolizes what the Avengers felt when they lost their friends and own families when the Snap happened—in an instant they were gone. The scene sets up the rest of the film, with the Avengers reuniting and working to bring their friends and families back and return the universe to its rightful state. When Scott Lang/Ant-Man returns from the quantum realm to post-Snap San Francisco, his frantic search to find his daughter Cassie similarly homes in on the importance-of-family theme. When he does find her, she is five years older, a teenager. Their emotional reunion has Scott emotionally overwhelmed, another instance of a male superhero showing love and affection. One might read this as foreshadowing that perhaps the Avengers can reverse the effects of the Snap and experience their own reunions with their families.

Particularly noticeable regarding Marvel's new man and the fulfillment of the parental role is how Tony Stark embraces fatherhood. In the five years since the Snap, he has retreated to a house in the country with his wife Pepper Potts, and they have a young daughter, Morgan. In the scenes early in the film that include Morgan, it is Tony who appears with her; he goes outside where she is playing to announce lunchtime, and also tucks her back into bed after she finds her way downstairs while he is conducting computer simulations of time travel. As he says good night, after teasing her that he'll sell all her toys if she doesn't go to sleep, she tells him, "I love you 3,000." In Tony's reaction, one sees the genuine love and gratitude a devoted father has for his child. In these domestic scenes, the viewer sees Tony participating in childcare, not as something special, but what appears to be his daily routine. This facet of Tony adds to his character arc, as he values his wife and daughter to the point of outright rejecting the idea of rejoining the Avengers in their mission to retrieve the Infinity Stones. However, it is his wife who persuades him to go help his friends to help others get their families back.

While the prioritization of family and involvement in parenting are obvious signals that contribute to a more progressive version of masculinity, the father–daughter motif in the personal storylines of Clint, Scott, and Tony adds another layer to *Endgame*'s portrayals of a feminist-leaning masculinity. Each of these fathers appears in key scenes with their daughters in particular, which one can read as forwarding a theme that the future is female. The continuation of the Avengers beyond *Endgame* and into the future alludes to perhaps a female-majority Avengers team. Clint teaches his daughter archery, his master skill. Early in the film, when Tony fetches his daughter Morgan for lunchtime, she is wearing the armored helmet he had crafted for his wife Pepper Potts; one could read this as foreshadowing a future Morgan Stark perhaps picking up his legacy and becoming a superhero in her own right. This future-is-female allusion becomes further punctuated by Thor's "handing over" the leadership of New Asgard to Valkyrie at the end of the film.[3] Whether or not these scenes suggest a dismantling of patriarchy in the MCU of the future in favor of superhero egalitarianism, they provide in some small way at least a glimmer of hope.

MARVEL'S NEW MEN: ASSEMBLE

A Gramscian perspective to filmmaking, and media production in general, in a capitalistic system requires one to acknowledge that what appears onscreen originates from the culture in which it not only is created but needs to appeal to in order to make a profit. While certainly unprofitable cultural products may receive attention and accolades, media industries rely on their audiences to survive. Even when a film or television program may appear as non-ideological, or even nonsensical, it relays a culture's way of life. As Comolli and Narboni (1976) asserted, "the majority of films in all categories are the unconscious instruments of the ideology which produces them" (p. 25). Thus, they contended, "every film is political," in that it is determined by that ideology (p. 24). When considered within this definitively Gramscian viewpoint, then, *Endgame*'s depictions of masculinity reflect not only the writers' ideas about how their characters should speak and behave but also how they think audiences would receive their cultural product (which often is determined by test screenings prior to a film's release). The final product as distributed, marketed, and consumed thus serves as a sort of barometer for measuring mediated versions of masculinity, and, concurrently, gender in a broader sense.

Endgame is a movie about comic book characters, and belongs definitively in the realm of popular culture, which Gramsci saw as an important site of cultural production. Full of action and a "feast for the eyes" (McCarthy, 2019), its appeal is measured by its astounding box-office success on a world-wide scale. Although observations regarding its artistic value may characterize it as "worldwide audiovisual entertainment" as compared to "cinema" (Scorsese, 2019), a Gramscian perspective sees *Endgame* nevertheless as cultural production, and its content deserves, and even requires, a critical examination regarding how it conveys a gender ideology. Our close reading of its content as related to Hollywood versions of manhood thus aligns with the goal of media literacy as helping us to learn from and detect deeper messages in cultural content beyond the immediate sensory experience. Indeed, we see *Endgame* as both audiovisual entertainment and cinema if cinema is indeed about "esthetic, emotional, and spiritual revelation," and emphasizes characters in terms of "complexity of people and their contradictory and sometimes paradoxical natures, the way they can hurt one another and love one another and suddenly come face to face with themselves," as explained by Scorsese (2019). *Endgame* enjoyed immense financial and critical success, and contains this complexity regarding its characters, explained Ordoña

(2019) in a defense of the film that cited the film's writers, other film directors associated with the MCU, and even mental health clinicians who noted its emotional intelligence.

"Cinema is one of the languages through which the world communicates itself to itself," declared Comolli and Narboni (1976, p. 25). The term "cinema" here is applied to all films, the previous commentary by Scorsese regarding what constitutes its genuine form notwithstanding. Through *Endgame*, its creators, who write from the perspective of their own culture, communicate that culture's notions of masculinity—including its hegemonic forms, as explained in the previous chapter—to the same culture, as well as to others through media globalization.

A close reading of *Endgame*'s central male characters using theories of hegemonic masculinity and normative male alexithymia resulted in identification of four themes that assemble into a version of masculinity that reflects much in the way that Gillam and Wooden (2008) described Pixar's new man. The new man as depicted in the Pixar universe began as alpha-male types, who learned the value of communal effort, empathy, and seeking help after experiencing defeat. In *Endgame*, which serves as a denouement to the MCU's Avengers films, Marvel's new man also experienced failure and humiliation after battling an extremely powerful enemy (who can be read as a metaphor for an immense and formidable challenge that anyone may have to face). Marvel's new man similarly displays traits that promote a less confined masculinity, and reflects an evolution toward a more progressive attitude that incorporates those behaviors coded as feminine.

In particular, our analysis offers four themes that relate to how male characters in *Endgame* encompass a range of behaviors that veer from traditional, hegemonic masculinity: seeking help from and giving help to others, emotional expressiveness, expressions of fear and vulnerability, and emphasis on father–child relationships reflective of the value placed on family over "work." Marvel's new man departs from earlier versions of superheroes who work alone, a function of the whole point of the teamwork implicit and explicit in the Avengers films. Reliance on others becomes even more pronounced throughout *Endgame* when characters—who have superpowers, remember—find themselves in need of others' assistance. What makes *Endgame* notable are the instances in which these male superheroes verbalize that they need help. The normalization of support groups as sites where help is given and received also adds to the normalization of men asking for and receiving help. In addition, support for the LGBTQIA+ community, as conveyed in the support group scene led by Steve Rogers, offers a counterpoint to the homophobic aspects of hegemonic masculinity.[4]

Verbalization of emotion and the range of emotions expressed by Marvel's new man throughout *Endgame* breaks from hegemonic masculinity and normative male alexithymia; demonstrations of affection by Steve, Tony, and Scott, for example, illustrate the beneficial aspects of displays of emotion. The communication between male characters can include intimate talk, even if framed as comic banter or not-so-subtle digs at one another, such as Tony's commentary about Steve's backside. This could be read as part of the pair's homoerotic subtext in the Avengers films (McGrath, 2016), or as an example of covert intimacy, which characterizes male–male friendships (Fixmer-Oraiz and Wood, 2019).

Scott's positive assessment of Steve's body, however, gives an additional dimension to the scene. His overt admiration for Steve throughout the film presents for viewers a sweetness that makes his character even more appealing and likable. As another facet of the persona of Marvel's new man, this only contributes to a more complete portrayal of not only masculinity but humanness in general. Although we found this example of the interaction between the characters as contributing to a more progressive treatment of the interaction between male friends, particularly Tony and Steve, Mohan (2019) observed the film could have done more. In the moments before Tony's death, for example, Steve is not with him to say goodbye to his friend. Mohan decried the limited treatment of the male characters' friendships, invoking a near-Gramscian critique of this aspect of the MCU: "It is disheartening to think that in 2019, when we are celebrating 11 years of a franchise, that close-minded capitalists can hinder something as simple as a bromance." Market forces and considerations of not pushing too far what audiences may find acceptable thus prevent a truly radical and counterhegemonic portrayal of true friendship between men onscreen.

Emotional expressiveness by men might break the mold of hegemonic masculinity, but the expression of fear, self-doubt, and vulnerability shatters it—and even more so when considering that *Endgame* and the MCU feature not only characters of strength and courage, but superheroes whose abilities are beyond those of any mere human. The superhero Avengers include not only humans but a Norse *god* (for Odin's sake!). In the story of Thor—who put his physical strength and bravery to the test when he took on the full power of star in *Avengers: Infinity War*—we find a god portrayed as especially vulnerable and emotionally damaged, which offers a metaphor that shows even the strongest of the strong sometimes cannot cope with failure and the loss of confidence. Further, his anxiety and ability to cry and express his need to seek comfort and reassurance from his mother make him human, and, hence, relatable. Although problematic, as Thor clearly could benefit from professional help, one can read his depiction as allowing the viewer to surmise that Thor needs such help, or at the very least should ask Steve for assistance in finding a support group. If the writers had depicted Thor getting some help, they would have taken that additional step that would make *Endgame* even more of an example of how Hollywood filmmaking can incorporate a prosocial message regarding mental health into even the most fantastical story. However, Brusuelas (2019) pointed out that these superheroes are not infallible, and that their problems have no right or wrong answers. In that Thor does manage to overcome his self-doubt and gather the inner strength to keep going and find his innate courage to join his friends in the fight of their lives, one can see a lesson in tenacity and not giving up, even when things look bleak. In this sense, the kind of strength that hegemonic masculinity requires of men becomes altered, molded into strength of character rather than brute strength or the need to dominate others.

Endgame's emphasis on family, however defined, was noted as a prominent theme by reviewers such as Debruge (2019). In terms of masculinity, the prioritization of work over family has marked cultural definitions of manhood in the era of industrialization, with childcare still relegated to women (Fixmer-Oraiz and Wood, 2019). In the film, the viewer sees Tony Stark in a nurturing role, taking care of his young daughter; his wife does not appear in those scenes. Not only does this show fathers can do childcare, but superhero dads can do it as well. Although he had given up his Iron Man identity, this aspect of Tony becomes part of his character arc, which leads him to display the ultimate love in the form of his self-sacrifice to end Thanos. The appearance of a father–daughter motif throughout the film, with Clint teaching his daughter archery and Scott reuniting with his daughter, adds another reading that alludes to the passing on of the father's legacy to his female child. Thor's handing over leadership of New Asgard to Valkyrie certainly mirrors this, hinting that perhaps the MCU might feature more women superheroes (or even villains).

When taken together, these themes tend toward "feminine" traits—emotional expressiveness, asking for and giving help, self-disclosure, and family centeredness and childcare. As these are out of line with hegemonic masculinity in its contemporary form, they pose a counterhegemony that challenges the gender status quo. Brusuelas (2019) argued that showing male characters addressing their emotions, thus essentially removing their mask of masculinity, reflects a feminist stance. The male superheroes in *Endgame* display physical strength, overcome self-doubt and grief, and ultimately win the battle and right the universe. At the same time, their masculinity incorporates non-masculine behaviors, ones that balance what could have been a manhood completely in line with the stereotype of the strong, silent hero who never shows fear and keeps his feelings in check. *Endgame*'s men do not suffer from normative male alexithymia, and thereby offer a model of masculinity that encourages open and honest communication without fear of looking unmanly. In this sense they are truly fearless.

The array of male characters' portrayals in *Endgame* illustrates Connell's (2001) explanation that definitions of masculinities are not absolute but unsettled and that "masculinities may have multiple possibilities concealed within them" (p. 19). Further, noted Connell, the openness of hegemony allows for gender patterns to change, in that the complexity surrounding those gender patterns serves as a source of tension that can lead to that change. Indeed, critics' reviews of *Endgame* noted the positive way in which it presented masculinity overall (Anthony, 2019; Carlson, 2019; Rojas, 2019). Anthony (2019), in praising the film for its depiction of its male characters, alluded to the possibilities for change as reflected in the way hegemony functions as the struggle between status quo and eventual social transformation: "Whether by design or not, the Marvel Cinematic Universe has become a powerful and fascinating exploration of what it means to be a good man, and the ever-changing nature of it. *Endgame* is the culmination of it." Rojas (2019) further noted how "Smart Hulk" in *Endgame* illustrates the melding of Bruce Banner's intelligence with his alter ego Hulk's brute strength—which "allowed him to integrate all the aspects of his personality," and thus become a "complete developed being." Indeed, "Smart Hulk" could serve as a metaphor for the benefits of incorporating and celebrating in each individual the range of gender-coded human emotions, behaviors, and mindsets rather than maintaining their separation on the basis of sex.

Further, taking a bird's eye view, one can read Thanos as representative of traditional/hegemonic masculinity that values independence, emotional stoicism, rationality (eliminating half the universe or even all of it to save it), brute strength, and a patriarchal, unilateral decision-making form of power. In opposition would be the Avengers style of masculinity which encompasses "non-masculine" traits such as communal cooperation, equality (both general and gender), and emotionality. How daughters are treated also becomes a site for oppositional difference, in how Thanos treats his two adopted daughters with more cruelty than nurturance, while the Avengers dads value and nurture their daughters. In this manner, *Endgame* offers multiple textual levels at which to analyze masculinity and its variants, as conveyed through cultural production.

Rojas (2019), writing about *Endgame*'s masculinity portrayals for the advocacy group New Jersey Coalition Against Sexual Assault (NJCASA), concluded, "Ultimately, the Avengers are stories about dedication to others, sacrifice, and protecting the vulnerable. These are all values consistent with healthy masculinity." The use of *Endgame* specifically as a media literacy tool highlights the beneficial aspects of popular culture entertainment. Rojas did point out some unhelpful portrayals, such as Clint's campaign of revenge after the Snap, but her overall assessment that the Avengers forwards a healthy version of manhood mirrors that of our deconstruction presented here. The need for a media literacy approach to reviewing films and other mass media becomes especially cogent when considering the purpose of NJCASA, which is to advocate on behalf of sexual assault victims and to support prevention strategies "that work to address and defy the socio-cultural norms that permit and promote rape culture" ("About us," 2021). One of the ways to defy those norms is through media literacy—and evaluating how media, and the MCU, perpetuate hegemonic thinking regarding gender. As NJCASA discloses (2019) and media literacy scholar and advocate Mary-Lou Galician (2019) noted, one can certainly enjoy the media they consume, but always with a critical eye and understanding of how media industries function and the messages cultural products contain beyond the story and characters we see onscreen.

Marvel's new man in many ways expands the universe of masculinity as defined in mass media and promotes healthy notions surrounding what it means to be a man, and, more importantly, a good man. The aggregate, although not completely unflawed, positive masculinity that appears in *Endgame* demonstrates that incursions into hegemony are possible. Not only are they possible, but one can view those incursions, as folded into popular culture products such as the MCU franchise, as ways to influence common-sense ideas centered on gender. Furthermore, projects such as this analysis of *Endgame* and the commentaries and reviews that abound online that take a serious look at entertainment contribute to a progressive movement toward how we can unlearn gender. "Research on the multiple forms of masculinity, for instance, may help people to recognize the diversity of masculinities, the open-ended possibilities in gender relations—and thus see alternatives for their own lives," wrote Connell (2001, p. 26).

Messerschmidt (2018) reiterated the potential for changing the status quo regarding gender status, hierarchy, and societal expectations. Conceptualizations of hegemonic masculinity, Messerschmidt wrote, "should acknowledge explicitly the possibility of *democratizing* gender relations and of abolishing power differentials—not just of reproducing hierarchy" (p. 57). Establishing a version of masculinity open to equality with women makes it possible to create positive masculinities, which "remain a key strategy for contemporary efforts at reform" (p. 57). In the case of *Endgame*, the overall masculinity presented—in the form of the male characters discussed here and how they display traits that push against hegemonic masculinity—certainly could be considered a positive version of masculinity, as opposed to those versions that emphasize strength, restrictive emotionality, and extreme self-reliance. In that the male Avengers work and fight alongside female superheroes as equals—and indeed rely on their women counterparts in times of need, as explained here—the film does appear to align with positive masculinity as described by Messerschmidt.

We must provide a caution to this optimistic assessment: However progressive these male superheroes appear in terms of their individual and aggregate masculinities, the film *itself* requires a closer look regarding whether or not it democratizes gender relations and works to eliminate power differentials. When considering the way the women superheroes are portrayed and treated in *Endgame*, hegemonic masculinity appears to have an edge over the resistance presented by Marvel's new man, as we discuss next.

ALAS, WHERE IS MARVEL'S NEW WOMAN?

Framing *Endgame* as a site of hegemonic struggle, we see this wildly popular cultural artifact as pushing against hegemonic masculinity yet paradoxically enabling a patriarchal ideology to remain emplaced. Jones (2017), in an online commentary, addressed the gender and diversity angles of the MCU, and observed women and men aren't given the same weight in the MCU and that its print comics contain more diversity than its onscreen products. Women in the MCU, Jones concluded, have limited roles reflective of traditional/hegemonic femininity: they are physically attractive, hold the "bare minimum" requirements to be considered a strong female archetype, and exist to be the heterosexual love interest of the men. As we have exposited here, *Endgame* features male characters who defy the conventional persona of the masculine male. If Marvel's new man presents a progression of men's onscreen portrayals, then what can be said about the way that the female superheroes similarly presents a progression of women's onscreen portrayals? Do the women in *Endgame* also break free of cultural notions of femininity and womanhood?

Alas, even as characters such as Natasha/Black Widow and Carol Danvers/ Captain Marvel, along with Nebula and Gamora, the adoptive daughters of Thanos, appear to be featured as major players in the narrative, and the epic battle contains an attention-grabbing (though rather short) all-woman superheroes scene, in aggregate the women still tend to play the "support staff" to the men. Rather than the central heroes who save the universe—such as Tony Stark, who makes the ultimate sacrifice—the women of *Endgame* help to advance the storyline, but are not vital to the plot. Indeed, their overall treatment as compared to the men received negative attention by online commentators and critics, who pointed out not only the supporting roles the women played, but the outright mistreatment of the lone female Avenger, Natasha/ Black Widow (Armitage, 2019; Brusuelas, 2019; Dana, 2019; Kang, 2019; NJCASA, 2019; Rao, 2019; Savyasachi, 2019; Siede, 2019).

Overall, the women of *Endgame* support the men, and still exhibit the caring, nurturing role as assigned to them via societal expectations. For example, Hope van Dyne/The Wasp is support to Scott Lang/Ant-Man, Pepper Potts is support to her husband Tony Stark/Iron Man in the battle scene at the end of the film, and it is Nebula who nurses Tony when they are adrift in space after the Snap. Regarding Pepper's support role to Tony, she appears at the battle in the armored suit created by Tony for her; she appears as kind of an "Iron Woman," and joins her husband in battle briefly as they literally have each other's back as they fight Thanos's hordes. In this sense, they appear to be equals—but, again, the scene is only a few seconds long. When Nebula tends to Tony, it calls to mind the nurturing role of women, especially mothers, and of the stereotypical female nurse tending to the sick. Rather than Tony, for example, tending to her, a woman, the trope of a woman tending to a man is shown; this reinforces the expectation of a woman playing "nurse" (and the commonsense expectation that nurses are female), and of having the innate skill to do so. If Tony had tended to a wounded Nebula, it would have enhanced his character's development, and his childcare role to his daughter.

The notable portion of the epic battle scene at the end of the film which has the women superheroes assembled together to run interference for Carol as she takes the Infinity Stones gauntlet and heads for Scott Lang's time machine gained much media attention, and rightfully so. The assemblage of the women—which included those who were taken at the Snap and suddenly reappear in time to join the battle—does have the visual impact to make an impression on the viewer. Siede (2019) commented that the brief scene served as "a big, showy salute to the female lineup" of the MCU, but nevertheless appeared "clunky," in that it "sacrifices all sense of internal logic in favor of simplistic iconography." Rao (2019), who similarly saw the scene as unhelpful in terms of advancing onscreen gender equality, called it "pandering," a "last-ditch effort" to address previous criticism about gender imbalance in the MCU. Kang (2019) called the all-woman battle scene "the apotheosis of the studio's expectation that fans of female superheroes be satisfied with scraps, while courting woke points for its supposed forward thinking." Brusuelas's (2019) verdict of the scene made a special point about how the women superheroes almost magically began working together as a team, even though it was the first time some of them had met: "This moment seems contrived, unnatural, and desperate. Remember, half of these characters don't even know each other," Brusuelas explained.

Adding to this largely negative evaluation, Siede (2019) termed the scene "glaringly patronizing," but found it at least offered a tribute to "the wildly talented real-life women who have spent years elevating thinly written roles through sheer force of will." Thus, while the image of a group of women banding together made for great visuals, a media literacy approach requires a re-thinking about how such a scene might obscure sense-making regarding its point within the context of not only the storyline but what these women superheroes are actually doing in the battle itself. This leads back to their utility as support personnel, rather than taking on key roles turning the tide of the battle and achieving victory. Further, these women superheroes still uphold hegemonic femininity through their physical appearance: they are beautiful, wear costumes that emphasize their body shape (none are anywhere near overweight), and there is no question that they are feminine females. They never look sweaty or dirty, as one would expect after fighting for hours.

In *Endgame*, the appearance of Carol Danvers/Captain Marvel at the beginning of the film as she rescues Tony Stark and Nebula from certain death reminds one of a savior "coming to the rescue." Her immense powers, which eclipse those of Tony Stark's Iron Man and Steve Rogers's Captain America, include space travel without the need for a vessel in addition to tremendous physical strength. However, even as she is perhaps the greatest of the MCU superheroes, she is still derided by "Rhodey" Rhodes/War Machine, who calls her "new girl" when she joins the Avengers at their headquarters after bringing Tony and Nebula back to Earth (Thor, on the other hand, welcomes her to the team). Five years later, during a check-in session with other Avengers allies convened by Natasha, Carol's new short hairstyle is mocked, emphasizing how women are often judged on their physical appearance over their brains (or, in this case, incredible powers). When Natasha asks if the team would be seeing her in the next month, Carol replies that it won't be likely. Rocket Raccoon then pipes up and says, "What? You're going to get another haircut?" Carol responds with a "diss" of her own, calling him "Furface" and explaining that she will be busy helping other planets across the universe that are undergoing crises similar to that experienced on Earth.

As mentioned previously, Steve Rogers/Captain America calls on Carol to help the team during the battle with Thanos and his legions. This hints at the notion that a man is relying on a woman for help—and acknowledging that she has the power to do so at such a crucial time. She is the only one of the superheroes who could physically grab hold of Thanos, yet in the final battle scene he is still able to repel her, leaving Tony to defeat Thanos. However, even Captain Marvel plays a supporting role in *Endgame*, which one can rationalize as being because she had a film all her own, the box-office hit *Captain Marvel* that was released in March 2019, the month prior to *Endgame*. However, her trivialized treatment in *Endgame*, being called "girl"—a term that infantilizes her—and the comment about her hair reinforces a gender hierarchy in which females are still relegated to a lower status than men. In this manner, even though the most powerful superhero in the MCU (Watercutter, 2019), she is cut down to size so as not to eclipse the MCU's men.

Of the problematic aspects of *Endgame* regarding women's status, the treatment of Natasha Romanova/Black Widow appears especially so, as noted in numerous reviews (Armitage 2019; Angus, 2019; Brusuelas, 2019;

NJCASA, 2019; Rao, 2019; Savyasachi, 2019; Siede, 2019). In the five years after the Snap, Natasha took on the leadership role for the Avengers while Tony went into seclusion with his family, Clint took on his own campaign of revenge, Thor sank into his depression, and Steve was involved in the support group. When the Avengers reunited for their time-travel mission to retrieve the Infinity Stones, she and Clint went to the planet of Morag to get the Soul Stone. As she and Clint struggled with each other to make the sacrifice required in order to get the stone, she ultimately won. Her self-sacrifice serves as a symbolic act that has gendered meaning. Because Clint had a (biological) family and she didn't, her death suggests that her worth was less than his—she does not have a biological family to take care of nor children of her own. In this manner, her inability to fulfill the traditional gender role of mother suggests she is "less than" a man who fulfills the role of father. In other words, the gender ideology that dictates if a woman does not have children, then she has failed as a woman becomes a way to rationalize why she dies and Clint does not. Further, her death is not marked with the ritual of a funeral. Rather, the remaining male Avengers discuss her death, and resolve to complete the mission.

When compared to Tony Stark's memorial service at the end of the film, which the MCU superheroes and related characters attend as a kind of curtain call for the franchise, the simple acknowledgment of Natasha's death—and thus her as an Avenger and person—seems almost paltry and even insignificant. Furthermore, if one approaches Natasha's narrative in the film in terms of the implicit message regarding women and leadership, her death comes after she has assumed a leadership role. Leadership in the United States historically has been associated with men rather than women, as reflected in the saying "think leader, think male." This becomes even more prominent when considering the continuing challenges women face as they seek political office and the paucity of women leaders in the business world.[5] Natasha's assumption of a leadership role in the aftermath of the Snap only to be followed by her self-sacrifice for the sake of the Avengers' ultimate mission thus could be read as reflective of the slow progress toward gender equality in the society in which *Endgame* was produced.

Regarding the "passing of the baton" theme from father to daughter mentioned earlier in this chapter, the final scenes of the film keep that theme from becoming overly obvious. When Steve Rogers returns from the past as an old man, he brings with him his Captain America shield and gives it to Sam Wilson/Falcon. This racially symbolic handing over of the identity of Captain America—a metaphor for the leadership of America (the United States)—to Sam, an African American man, could be read as a progressive gesture indicating that the person to represent "America" is nonwhite. However, in that a woman was not handed the legacy also could be read in terms of a reminder of the 2008 U.S. presidential race, when Barack Obama and Hillary Clinton competed against each other, with Obama winning. When also considered in the context of the 2016 presidential campaign and Hillary Clinton's loss in a contest with a lesser qualified, male candidate, *Endgame*'s ending reinforces the societal expectation that leadership is for men, rather than women. In this manner, just enough of the text hints at the transformation of patriarchy, with this last element—the passing on of Captain America's legacy—preventing a dismantling that would threaten the current state of affairs.

CONCLUSION

A Gramscian perspective of the study of popular culture considers films like those in the Marvel Cinematic Universe a view into a culture—its values, ways of thinking, and commonsense notions regarding facets of everyday life. Here, we applied hegemony theory to an analysis of the 2019 film *Avengers: Endgame*, relying on hegemonic masculinity as a lens through which we closely read its text to identify how the film's male characters interrupt dominant versions of masculinity. The dialectical nature of masculinity, Connell (2001) pointed out, makes it dynamic. In turn, the recognition of the dynamics of masculinity is "to acknowledge that particular masculinities are composed, historically, and may also be de-composed, contested, and replaced" (p. 20).

Throughout the film, the incorporation of feminine-coded behaviors displayed through the onscreen portrayals of male characters that run counter to hegemonic masculinity as reviewed in chapter 4, "Hegemonic Masculinity in the Mass Media," presents a revised male superhero persona we dub Marvel's new man. This new man, rather than exhibiting the self-reliance, emotional reserve, and brave face expected of masculine men, asks for and accepts help from others, expresses his feelings, and admits self-doubt. An emphasis on familial themes and of the display of love—both of selfless, altruistic love known as *agape* and of familial love known as *storge*—also mark *Endgame*'s appeal to pathos.[6]

Emotionality—both on the part of the characters in the text and that of viewers—takes the film beyond the typical action film. A motif of father–daughter relationships also become highlighted, as the dad superheroes are shown at home with their children. Glimmers of a feminist theme, aside from the unmasking of the masculine front that allowed for these men to show their humanness, occasionally shine through, as allusions to their daughters' taking up their legacy were detected as well.

The overall healthy masculinity portrayal offered in *Endgame*, as Rojas (2019), writing for the New Jersey Coalition Against Sexual Violence

(NJCASA), noted, unfortunately appears not to accompany a portrayal of the women superheroes that shows them in an equally positive way. A follow-up essay to Rojas's treatment of the way *Endgame* portrays the men on the Avengers team titled "Breaking Down the Boys' Club" (NJCASA, 2019) highlighted that MCU films can be enjoyed, but that media literacy skills are needed to assess how these popular media "continue to reflect norms that devalue women's work, objectify them, and place them in supportive roles to male characters." Herein lies the site at which hegemonic struggle plays out between the resistive version of masculinity presented by *Endgame* and the status quo of gender relations, in which women still present traits and behaviors coded not only as feminine but also coded as being of lesser status to men. In this sense, hegemonic masculinity might appear as being challenged at the level of the portrayals of male characters in *Endgame*, but in that hegemonic masculinity really is all about unequal gender relations, its power tilts toward the status quo. In short, the men onscreen might be changing in a progressive direction, but the women continue to be treated in a way that upholds inequality in gender status.

However, ever in the spirit of hegemony's openness that allows for incursions of counterhegemony that eventually lead to change, the potential for future offerings that focus on women superheroes such as Captain Marvel pose opportunities for a more female-forward path for the MCU. Hence, the potential for further progress in terms of gender egalitarianism, whether in the form of modifications to masculinity or the equal treatment of men and women superheroes—wherein characters' fulfillment of assigned gender roles plays no part in their fate—is always present. Of course, a greater challenge to the fruition of onscreen changes depends on the progress occurring within the film industry itself.

This presents another facet of hegemony theory and the ways in which it functions in "real life," as Hollywood continues to face scrutiny regarding its power structure. Ever-present market considerations in a capitalistic economic system also prevent more radical changes in cultural production. The male superheroes are still muscular and exert physical strength. Violence retains validity as a course of action when dealing with villains. And gender differences remain that signify who can "save the universe" and who must still look feminine and attractive even as she participates in combat. The status quo still holds sway, and the threat of a complete overturning of the division between masculine and feminine is held definitively at bay. Incursions into the stability of civil society are just enough to make only the slightest dent, allowing a small amount of "counter" to the gender hegemony that is being challenged through culture products that dabble with the tried-and-true formula so present for so long in Hollywood.

Beyond analyses of specific texts in and of themselves, future research of the superhero genre and of the MCU might benefit from comparative studies that examine differences and similarities between film genres and even between the production arms of the same media company. For example, we borrowed from Gillam and Wooden's (2008) analysis of Pixar and its new man persona to look at how male characters in *Endgame* offer revisions to hegemonic masculinity as depicted in mass media. As both Pixar and Marvel are owned by the same corporation, the Walt Disney Company, one might approach the topic of mediated masculinity in terms of how their combined media products reflect a particular point of view regarding gender. Are characters that appear in Pixar and Marvel films gender progressive or not? What is the gender composition within the power structure at each of these production houses? What thematic content do these two components of a major media conglomeration have in common? These questions serve only as springboards for projects that ultimately aim to promote critical thinking on the part of both media consumers and creators.

NOTES

1. Christopher Markus and Stephen McFeely wrote the screenplay for *Avengers: Endgame*. Reference citation for quoted material in this chapter: Markus, C., McFeely, S. (Writers), & Russo, A., Russo, J. (Directors). (2019). *Avengers: Endgame* [Motion picture]. Marvel Studios.

2. Steve Rogers/Captain America had previous experience with support groups in *Captain America: The Winter Soldier* (2014), when he attended a support group for military veterans run by his friend Sam Wilson/Falcon, who also is a military veteran (Tyler, 2019).

3. Even the Avengers' villain Thanos has daughters, rather than sons.

4. The support group inclusion of the "grieving man," played by *Endgame* director Joe Russo, gained media attention, in that it was the first time an openly gay character appeared in the MCU films (Ahlgrim, 2019; Baggs, 2019).

5. Research on gender and leadership spans across academic disciplines, and comprises its own field of study. See Valian's *Why So Slow?* (1999) for more on women and leadership. Studies that have analyzed perceptions of leadership include those by Jackson, Engstrom, and Emmers-Sommer (2007) on young people's perception of gender and leadership; Lawless and Fox (2004) on gender imbalance in politics; and Molintas (2020) on gender and leadership in the hospitality industry, to name only a few.

6. *Agape* characterizes the self-sacrifice made by Tony Stark and Natasha as they gave their lives for the greater good. *Storge* appears in the form of how the Avengers feel as if they were family, as expressed by Natasha to Steve. Both types originate in the ancient Greek conceptions of love, as summarized by Galician (2019).

Chapter 6

Conclusion

"Instead of a Gramscian legend we now have Gramsci's legacy in the form of books—even though he never actually wrote any books," wrote Buttigieg (1986, p. 3). More than thirty years after this observation, Gramsci's writings continue to hold relevance. By adding another contribution to the range of books (and articles) written about and inspired by Gramsci, we aimed to illuminate the evergreen ideas he left behind that addressed the role of mass media as a cultural producer of both hegemonic and counterhegemonic thought. As tools for uncovering, deconstructing, and reassembling ideologies contained within media messages, media literacy offers us a way to critically ponder the ways in which common sense becomes common. How to turn that common sense into good sense, however, presents a challenge to those of us who desire, as did Gramsci, a world in which egalitarianism, social justice, and the dignity of the individual become reified as their own composite hegemonic thought and practice.

Just as Gramsci saw education as an equalizing and exigent component of society, we see media literacy as crucial, especially now with the vast array of media offerings Gramsci could not possibly have foreseen. To the extent that any piece of media supports the moment's hegemony, media literacy teaching and criticism offer counterhegemonic ways of thinking. The advantage comes with a newfound, deeper ability to understand the material circumstances in which one finds oneself. We explored the media literacy tools that people can use through the practices of cultural studies, which seeks a ground-up way of approaching media texts and identifies the politics involved in consumption. The 1970s film *Soldier Blue* and HBO's *Watchmen* and *Lovecraft Country* serve as examples of texts that have the potential of offering antiracist stories that could contribute to the struggle against the coercive force of hegemony. But these are always subject to the transformations in culture as it responds

111

to new circumstances and potentially a new culture, while always being wary of the power of existing corporate media industries to reclaim that ground and dismantle the anti-hegemonic through the power of the current hegemony and its efforts to dominate education, media, and any other ideological apparatus that contests for power.

However, even as we as media consumers can pick and choose where and how we get our information—whether as news, educational content, or entertainment—the modifier "simple" preceding the act of choosing and the act of obtaining belies the intricate production processes involved in bringing that information to us through our smartphones, computers, and TVs. Regardless of the mode of mass communication, we cannot simply let those messages wash over us without giving thought to the process by which it came to us. As we noted throughout this book, we can enjoy our media while also thinking of them critically.

Our case study of entertainment media in the form of the highly popular and entertaining Hollywood film *Avengers: Endgame* addressed this tenet of media literacy, and we approached it with Natharius's (2004) axiom that encapsulates its purpose: "The more we know, the more we see." The Grasmcian-based concept of hegemonic masculinity—the prevailing, composite traits associated with manhood most commonly depicted in cultural products—served as the "more we know" part. When armed with this knowledge, the consumption of a film designed to (1) make money while (2) entertaining its audiences becomes a means by which we "see" how cultural ideology surrounds and permeates that viewing experience.

By deconstructing gender ideology reflected in dialogue and action, we argued how hegemonic struggle between prevailing notions of masculinity and incursions presented by counterhegemonic portrayals lend to a reading of "maleness" that incorporates a "femaleness" associated with feminine-typed characteristics. Marvel's "new man" offers the potential and possibility for cultural producers to move beyond gendered stereotypes—and find tremendous economic success at the same time. However, we found that with such progress, movement toward an equally promising persona for Marvel's "new woman" appeared, at least in this film, less apparent.

This parallels the oftentimes inchmeal progress of wider society, wherein cultural changes occur gradually. As critical media consumers, our power comes in the form of rewarding progressive media through our demand for it, but as educators, we also must demonstrate to our students the benefits for them to "vote" with their own economic resources. Eventually, economic success of such media will become so great as to impel cultural producers, and the corporate machinery behind them, to manufacture narratives and images imbued with fresh ideologies that reflect a new "common sense." That common sense, we hope, will include the unquestioned belief in the equality of all human beings, and the notion that "gender" and its accompanying "rules" may someday be something from the ancient past.

However, the commercial media system, with its deep ties to global capitalism, has shown itself to be shrewd in adapting to a new common sense, without really changing the fundamental undercurrents that keep the power hierarchy in place. Consider the challenge presented by the vast range of representations of police officers in film and television. There should be broad and deep conversations about the social and cultural meaning of these representations, which are often harder to decode than most viewers think. In a January 18, 2021, public radio interview for the program *Here and Now*, show host Tonya Mosley spoke to actor Wendell Pierce, who played Detective Bunk Moreland in the 2002–2008 HBO series *The Wire*:

Mosley: Over the summer after the killing of George Floyd and Brianna Taylor, a lot of folks were re-watching and re-examining *The Wire*, where you played Baltimore police detective Bunk Moreland, and you said during that time that the drama, quote, "demonstrated moral ambiguities and the pathologies that leads to abuses, and that ultimately *The Wire* is art, and art is meant to ignite the public discourse." This is a big question I'm about to ask you, but in light of what happened over the summer and this last week's insurrection, what discussion about policing in America do you think we need to be having at this moment?

Pierce: It is a big question, Tonya . . .

Mosley: I know.

Pierce: . . . and rightfully so. Someone wrote to me, when we were having these discussions this summer, and said, "You were part of *The Wire*, and you celebrated that whole idea of policing, and the way the police come into our communities. You celebrated it." And I said, +If you look at *The Wire*, and you didn't see it as a condemnation of the systems that are oppressing people, you missed the point." And it made me realize, we really have to have a conversation. If you look at *The Wire*, and you see it as a celebration of policing instead of the condemnation of all of its dysfunction, then we really have a problem because we didn't get here overnight. It was an evolution of a mentality that goes all the way back to America's Original Sin. ("Actor Wendell Pierce," 2018)

In this exchange, Pierce points out how even a text as carefully constructed as *The Wire* can be misunderstood. Its intentions to critique are opposed by the inertia of film and television stories that do celebrate policing, especially aggressive policing that aligns with the desires of the audience to see the repressive power of the state—the police—as an agent working in the best interests of the public at large, maintaining "law and order."

Against this power, the critique that is written through *The Wire* can offer support only if the audience is willing to consider the complicated relationship between state power and the public, especially when race is part of the situation. The viewer in a position of privilege, particularly where privilege is unexamined, may misunderstand the critique. Commercial media industries have a great deal of experience making small shifts in content and language that appeal to the audience's desire for social justice, but never to the level of disrupting the basic functioning of the capitalist corporate media system. As the storylines adjust to new social pressures, the possibilities within the hegemonic order are renegotiated, but rarely does that renegotiation disrupt the hegemony significantly. The operation of the corporate commercial market is even given the status of a free and democratic marketplace of ideas. The choices among offerings are still limited by the offerings available in a corporate commercial media space. But can these limitations be disrupted in the digital and social media reality?

A GRAMSCIAN PERSPECTIVE ON
DIGITAL MEDIA LITERACY

Recent developments in the digital environment challenge many of the ways legacy media operated and continue to operate, both in terms of economics and in terms of the politics of popular culture. It is easy to reduce the changes in media culture to technological developments, but by doing so one can often overlook the desires that cultural members have to not just consume the products of professional media industries but also find ways of communicating in a new culture with a new way of feeling and seeing reality. The possibilities of dialogic communication in the digital media environment are very appealing to cultures that desire better ways to participate in public media spaces—though we also need to keep in mind how many of those public spaces are quite literally privately owned digital spaces, with a split obligation between private interests (for profit and growth) and a brand identity that disguises that aspect of their operation.

Gramsci would likely find both promise and dangers in the expanded interactive media environment, created and distributed through the digital sphere. This pluralism has the potential to allow for the creation and distribution of a vast range of new forms of expression. Some of this is accomplished through cheap access to the tools of production. Though entering the realm of digital production still has a cost, it is certainly not as prohibitive as it once was. Most mobile phones are capable of producing photographic, video, and audio quality at a level that will engage with viewers and listeners through the digital network. In other words, the audience is both producing content that bridges the gap between professional and amateur, in what Leadbeater referred to as the "Pro-Am Revolution" (2004), and seeking out that content under a whole new set of cultural standards. Serial narrative fiction stories are being constructed and delivered online, without any additional cost beyond the time it takes to get online and watch (see, e.g., the YouTube series *Marble Hornets* and *Don't Hug Me I'm Scared*). Today, the digital sphere offers a wide variety of audio stories told using the architecture of online podcasting, such as the "weird fiction" podcast *Welcome to Night Vale* and the audio drama *Bronzeville*.

But these remain transformative times for these media, and much like the capacity of hegemony to re-absorb anti-hegemonic media, these "Pro-Am" forms will face the struggles of being re-corporatized. A favorite form of storytelling that has been "acquired" by a larger media conglomerate can be a cause for celebration. But it also should be a cautionary moment, in that successful media producers take ideas that might have liberatory potential and turn them into a media product dominated by hegemonic storytelling. Thanks to their massive reach, large media corporations often follow paths that use massive transmedia structures to monetize creativity.

Gramsci brings to this complex media environment the importance of our awareness that hegemony involves a negotiation in which participants—whether creators or audiences, whether corporate professionals or Pro-Am participants—take part in the process, whether by advancing the interrogation of oppressive ideological constructions or going online to participate in the organic intellectual process of increasing awareness of material historical conditions and how they are represented. The privilege that puts people in the position of creating and distributing counterhegemonic representations ought to be called to account, noted Reed (2012), as well as the awareness that this process ties together media and education.

We see a desperate need for a Gramscian conversation that addresses the way emerging media forms work on us, considering the differences between how completely we understand media that had a major impact on culture before the digital revolution, and the newer media that accelerate at a pace that far outstrips the amount of time available to understand not just how a tool or an app works, but what it means when a culture develops a new media practice without a clear understanding of the consequences of that use. How much time does it take to develop a critical, reflexive, media literate understanding of what a particular kind of media use means for the user?

We also might consider all of the tumult surrounding the commodification of personal information across social media platforms. The sale and misuse of personal information to social media resulted from a lack of understanding on the part of individuals regarding how social media companies and website owners harvest and use this data. Users of social media often do not understand that all of the things they do online become data points, a commodity that the private social media businesses can sell. Users might even be notified about these uses, but the language is frequently buried in lengthy user agreements that almost no users read—by design.

For example, information about friends of users who did not even have Facebook accounts became commodified, bought, and then sold by Facebook. People understand even less the level of surveillance that happens regularly in current media culture, where browsers and histories, online searches, clicks and "likes" all contribute to a mountain of data that contains information both specific to the individual user and generalized into algorithms—the programs that react to what an individual does in interacting with the media and gives feedback in the form of suggestions, recommendations, and sales contacts. Often, users barely understand the influence of these algorithms that affect their decision making. Data scientist Cathy O'Neill discussed just how out of control algorithms have become in an article in the free digital news publication *Quartz* (Sonnad, 2016). Between the way online companies collect data—whether good data or bad data—and the way measures of success for the algorithm work, users again become caught in systems they do not understand.

From the perspective of media literacy, we need to realize that users do not need to understand how algorithms work any more than they need to understand electromagnetism in order to use a radio. But the consequences of not knowing have severely detrimental consequences. An algorithm you don't understand might just give a suggestion for the next song for you to listen to, based on your past selections, but it also might suggest the next video to watch, which has a bit more extreme point of view than the one you are currently watching. And gradually, unnoticeably, and imperceptibly, the user becomes subtly manipulated down the line toward radicalization, because the measure of an algorithm's success relies on the user to keep watching, keep paying attention, and then falling further down the rabbit hole.

Sitting next to this problem of users understanding how their media experience works we see the more pressing problem of how people respond to the complexity of a media environment stuffed with a proliferation of false and misleading information. While much has already been written about the consequences of such a media environment, addressing this would take another book-length work to discuss Gramsci and the information society. At the very least, Gramsci's ideas would hold out hope for a more successful collective struggle against a hegemony that in many ways wants to use fear and confusion as a means to alienate people from knowing their collective best interests. That may mean postponing the satisfaction that comes from simply following an individual's confirmation bias, and not falling into the trap of a feeling of powerlessness.

Counterhegemony, these basic propositions suggest, involves the practice of moral and intellectual leadership, which requires persuading and educating everyone in the process. Gramsci also suggests we rely on the critical learning dynamic that exists between the student (who is both student and teacher) and her teacher (who is both teacher and student). Moral and intellectual leadership—counterhegemony—also involves a process that requires educating the intellectual (or teacher), and moving the educational process itself beyond the abstract realm of the intellectual, that is, beyond a strictly scholastic relationship.

As educators, we must make knowledge historically meaningful by incorporating the raw experience of lived capitalist historicity into our teaching. "Intellectuals are, therefore, educated by interacting with the subaltern, whose feeling-passion informs their abstract understanding of reality" (Reed, 2012, p. 572). Through a shared cultural history that starts with folklore and common sense, moves through the traditions of legacy media storytelling such as film and television, and now experiences fundamental revolutions in the networked digital environment, the point becomes clearer over and over again: Communication among groups through the media exists as a fragile set of relationships that require the political commitment to look, to listen, and to converse (through different media). The conditions of power and capital need to match an interest in empowering marginalized and subaltern groups to become part of the media conversation, which means taking part in the struggle as well.

The networked social media environment offers tools that might encourage democratic and egalitarian participation, but using them for counterhegemonic purposes usually means a race against the clock. The ability to organize a collective action that questions the current regimes of power has great potential in the networked digital sphere. What once existed as the passive consumption of information and entertainment now offers the possibility of collective, creative collaboration. Fan fiction, the sharing of photos and images, the creation of stories shot on mobile phones and edited with free or inexpensive software tools, podcasts recorded and distributed on simple computers or iPhones—these and other soon-to-be-available media hold powerful potential, but their creators need to understand their use, meaning, and purpose. Consider the way anyone now can use cameras and mics in cell phones to turn the lens on the agents of power. Of course, most users need to understand the power of editing, and the potential for a sound or an image to become decontextualized in a way that promotes impatience and confusion. We have argued in this book for a strong, deep relationship between Gramsci's ideas about power and hegemony and the potential that lies in media literacy and critical education in general to not only question them, but counteract them.

CODA

The interrelationships between economics, race, gender, and class still need attention when it comes to equal access to education, much less equal access to media literacy training, both for students and for teachers. There remain places in the world where girls are restricted or prohibited from being educated in the same way that boys are restricted from stepping outside the hegemonic masculinity norms they learn through socialization. Access to education remains a financial challenge for families in many parts of the world. And the technologies that support education still pose a barrier, whether one considers the quality of learning materials available, or the "digital divide" that differentiates access to media through a digital network that adequately meets the needs of learners and teachers.

Educational efforts in the form of curricula that not only include but require courses in media literacy abound today, almost a century since Gramsci pondered the role of media in the struggle to attain what he called "praxis" (the realization of socialism). We strive as educators to attain for our students, and ourselves, the realization that mass media can have a purpose beyond the financial within a capitalist system—which appears to remain in place for the foreseeable future, at least in the United States. Media literacy taught both in survey courses that address critical consumption in general and courses that explore specific topics—like portrayals of gender, race, class, professions, and even love and romance—that lend themselves to media analysis and critique carry on Gramsci's legacy.[1]

Media consumers span the age range, and so does the need for media literacy. Although we wrote this book for media scholars and for students learning about mass communication at institutions of higher learning, media literacy can start when schooling starts. Founded in 1997, the National Association for Media Literacy Education mentioned in chapter 2 offers K-12 educators resources for teaching children to think critically about the media they encounter, which begins by asking questions (NAMLE, n.d.). "Question the media you love" serves as a motto of Feminist Frequency, a nonprofit media literacy organization founded in 2009 that analyzes media treatment of gender, race, and sexuality. Feminist Frequency's series of YouTube videos and podcasts feature deconstructions of popular media, including newly released and older films, video games, and news coverage of current events.[2] Also in keeping with Gramsci, its vision statement specifies its goal to create a "media landscape that fosters a just and equitable world for all people" ("About," 2009–2020). These efforts—available to anyone with access to the internet—reflect a Gramscian perspective in that they promote the need for a deeper, informed critique of seemingly innocuous messages that pervade the contemporary media environment.

Antonio Gramsci's vision of the media as conduits to effect social change continues to inspire, inform, and invigorate the study of mass culture. Mass media artifacts serve as a collective site where ideology becomes reified through narratives, character portrayals, dialogue, and visuals. Gramsci saw popular culture as legitimate as high art, and worthy of being treated as such. We hope we have shown here that worldwide audiovisual entertainment aimed at mass audiences serves as an apt and engaging conduit for applying Gramsci's notions about culture, ideology, and media literacy. We have little doubt that a Gramscian perspective, and even Gramsci himself, would want to develop counterhegemonic tools for the online media user, perhaps in a formal educational setting like a media literacy classroom, or perhaps in direct communication with people who seek and want greater control over the way media works *for* them and not just *on* them.

NOTES

1. University offerings include courses in information literacy that bring a media-critical approach to the study of popular culture and those specifically focused on media and digital literacy. Examples include the University of Kentucky's College of Communication and Information courses ICT/IS 200: Information Literacy & Critical Thinking and COM 453: Mass Media and Digital Literacy, taught in the School of Information Science and Department of Communication, respectively (we thank Kari Benguria and Don Lowe for providing course syllabi). For educators, Harvard University's Graduate School of Education offers the online workshop "Screen-Time Savvy: Skills and Strategies to Deepen Digital and Media Literacy" (https://online-learning.harvard.edu/course/screen-time-savvy-skills-and-strategies-deepen-digital-and-media-literacy).

2. Feminist Frequency can be found at https://www.youtube.com/user/feminist-frequency. *Avengers: Endgame* served as the topic for a podcast, evidencing its rich heuristic provocativeness as a popular culture artifact imbued with cultural meaning regarding fat shaming, queer representation, and the "feminist" moment in the film as discussed in chapter 5.

Bibliography

About—Feminist Frequency. (2009–2020). https://feministfrequency.com/about/

About us. (2021). NJCASA. https://njcasa.org/about/

Actor Wendell Pierce on the role of art in advancing social progress. (2021, January 18). [Radio recording]. https://www.wbur.org/hereandnow/2021/01/18/wendell-pierce-the-wire-police

Acu, A. (2016). The Marvel cinematic universe and the organized superhero. *Journal of Popular Film and Television*, *44*, 195–205.

Agresta, M. (2013, July 24). How the Western was lost (and why it matters). *The Atlantic*. https://www.theatlantic.com/entertainment/archive/2013/07/how-the-western-was-lost-and-why-it-matters/278057/

Ahlgrim, C. (2019, April 26). Avengers directors teased the debut of Marvel's first openly gay character in *Endgame*, but it wasn't at all what we expected. *Insider*. https://www.insider.com/avengers-endgame-first-openly-gay-character-joe-russo-scene-2019-4

Althusser, L. (1971). *Lenin and philosophy, and Other Essays*. Monthly Review Press.

American Psychological Association. (2020). Contact comfort, *APA dictionary of psychology*. dictionary.apa.org/contact-comfort

Angus, H. (2019, June 10). Black Widow and Captain Marvel: The duality of gender in the MCU. *Medium*. https://medium.com/@hanxine/black-widow-and-captain-marvel-the-duality-of-gender-in-the-mcu-80ac65aa94b3

Anthony, N. (2019, May 2). *Avengers: Endgame* is a culmination of what it means to be a man in the Marvel Cinematic Universe. *Medium*. https://medium.com/swish/avengers-endgame-is-a-culmination-of-what-it-means-to-be-a-man-in-the-marvel-cinematic-universe-1e9feb10690a

Apple, M. W. (1979). *Ideology and curriculum*. Routledge.

Arellano, L. (2015). The heroic monster: Dexter, masculinity, and violence. *Television and New Media*, *16*, 131–147.

Armitage, H. (2019, April 29). *Avengers: Endgame* fails the MCU's female characters AGAIN. *Digital Spy*. https://www.digitalspy.com/movies/a27285123/avengers-endgame-black-widow-nebula-female-characters/

Arnot, M. (1982). Male hegemony, social class and women's education. *Journal of Education, 164*, 64–89.

Artz, B. L. (2018). Global media practices and cultural hegemony. In S. Coban (ed.), *Media, ideology and hegemony* (pp. 4–40). Brill.

Artz, L., & Murphy, B. O. (2000). *Cultural hegemony in the United States*. Sage.

Asher-Perrin, E. (2013, May 17). *Supernatural*'s Dean Winchester dismantled his own machismo—and that's why we love him. *Tor.com*. http://www.tor.com/blogs/2013/05/supernaturals-dean-winchester-dismantled-his-own-machismo-and-thats-why-we-love-him

Askew, R. (2001). *Fire in Beulah*. Penguin Books.

Atkinson, J., & Calafell, B. (2009). Darth Vader made me do it! Anakin Skywalker's avoidance of responsibility and the gray areas of hegemony masculinity in the *Star Wars* universe. *Communication, Culture and Critique, 2*, 1–20.

Avengers: Endgame. (n.d.). https://www.boxofficemojo.com/release/rl3059975681/

Baggs, M. (2019, May 10). Endgame's gay moment: Why Marvel's next move may be an LGBT adventure. *Newsbeat*. https://www.bbc.com/news/newsbeat-48133076

Baldwin, J. (1965, March 7). The America dream and the American Negro. *The New York Times*, https://movies2.nytimes.com/books/98/03/29/specials/baldwin-dream.html.

Bates, T. (2002). Grasmci and the theory of hegemony. In J. Martin (ed.), *Antonio Gramsci: Critical assessments of Leading Political Philosophers* (Vol. 2) (pp. 245–262). Routledge.

Bauman, Z. (2000). *Liquid modernity*. Polity Press.

Beadling, L. (2016). Subverting the master's hero: *Firefly*'s Malcolm Reynolds as a feminist inflected space cowboy. In E. Abele & J. A. Gronbeck-Tedesco (eds.), *Screening images of American masculinity in the age of postfeminism* (pp. 69–82). Lexington.

Bean, T. (2020, April 24). All 24 Marvel Cinematic Universe films ranked at the box office—including *Black Widow*. *Forbes*. https://www.forbes.com/sites/travisbean/2020/04/24/all-23-marvel-cinematic-universe-films-ranked-at-the-box-office-including-black-widow/

Beliveau, R. (2011). 'You are reading too much into it': Using media criticism and production to develop student 'voice' and critical skills. *Journal of Media Education, 2*(2), 41–47.

Blumberg, A. T. (2014, October 21). My college classroom crusade to teach Marvel undergraduates. *The Conversation*. https://theconversation.com/my-college-classroom-crusade-to-teach-marvel-to-undergrads-32200

Boon, K. (2005). Heroes, metanarratives, and the paradox of masculinity in contemporary Western culture. *Journal of Men's Studies, 13*, 301–312.

Boukala, S. (2019). *European identity and the representation of Islam in the Mainstream Press: Argumentation and Media Discourse*. Palgrave Macmillan.

Bourdieu, P. (2000). *Pascalian meditations*. Stanford University Press.

Bourdieu, P. (2013). *Outline of a theory of practice*. Cambridge University Press.

Bové, P. (1994). Foreword. In M. Landy, *Film, politics and Gramsci* (pp. ix–xxii). University of Minneapolis Press.

Briziarelli, M., & Guillem, S. M. (2016). *Reviving Gramsci: Crisis, communication, and change*. Routledge.

Briziarelli, M., & Karikari, E. (2016). Antonio Gramsci and communication studies. *Oxford research encyclopedia of communication*. [Online]. Oxford University Press. doi: 10.1093/acrefore/9780190228613.013.78

Brueggeman, N. (2019, October 23). Why Tulsa massacre depictions are more horrific than past portrayals of racial violence. *Medium*. https://medium.com/an-injustice/why-tv-depictions-of-the-tulsa-massacre-are-so-disturbing-73fbf4a83219.

Brusuelas, C. (2019, May 10). *Avengers: Endgame*—Marvel feminist reviews. *Medium*. https://medium.com/@cbrucewillis/avengers-endgame-marvel-feminist-reviews-82a2f38ff074

Burbules, N. C., & Berk, R. (1999). Critical thinking and critical pedagogy: Relation, differences, and limits. In T. S. Popkewitz & L. Fenler, (eds.), *Critical theories in education* (pp. 45–66). Routledge.

Buttigieg, J. (1986). The legacy of Antonio Gramsci. *boundary 2*, *14*(3), 1–17.

Buttigieg, J. (2002). On Gramsci. *Daedalus*, *131*(3), 67–70.

Carragee, K. M. (1993). A critical evaluation of debates examining the media hegemony thesis. *Western Journal of Communication*, *57*, 330–348.

Carlson, G. M. (2020, May 4). 5 best guy movies featuring positive masculinity. *Dudefluencer*. https://dudefluencer.com/best-guy-movies-featuring-positive-masculinity/

Collins, E., Jensen, M., Kanev, P., & MacCalla, M. (2004). Shifting power: US hegemony and the media. *Interdisciplinary Journal of International Studies*, *2*, 21–49.

Connell, R. W. (2001). Understanding men: Gender sociology and the new international research on masculinities. *Social Thought Research*, *24*, 13–31.

Connell, R. W., & Messerschmidt, J. W. (2005). Hegemonic masculinity: Rethinking the concept. *Gender & Society*, *19*, 829–859.

Comolli, J. -L., & Narboni, J. (1976). Cinema/ideology/criticism. In B. Nichols (ed.), *Movies and methods* (Vol. 1) (pp. 22–30). University of California Press.

Connor, J. (2020, February 20). The 1921 Tulsa race massacre will officially become a part of Oklahoma school curriculum beginning in the fall. *The Root*. https://www.theroot.com/the-1921-tulsa-race-massacre-will-officially-become-a-p-1841814944

Crehan, K. (2016). *Gramsci's Common Sense: Inequality and Its Narratives*. Duke University Press.

Dana. (2019, May 6). *Avengers: Endgame* [Film review]. *Mediaversity Reviews*. https://www.mediaversityreviews.com/film-reviews/2019/5/6/avengers-endgame

Day, R. (2005). *Gramsci is dead: Anarchist current in the Newest Social Movements*. Pluto Press.

De Beukelaer, C., Pyykkönen, M., & Singh, J. (eds.). (2015). *Globalization, culture and development: The UNESCO convention on Cultural Diversity*. Palgrave.

Debruge, P. (2019, April 20). *Avengers: Endgame*. [Film review]. *Variety*, pp. 71–72.

Deer, C. (2012). Doxa. In M. Grenfell (ed.), *Pierre Bourdieu: Key concepts* (2nd ed.), (pp. 114–125). Acumen.

Dombroski, R. (1986). On Gramsci's theater criticism. *boundary 2, 14*(3), 91–117.

Dundes, A. (ed.) (1999). *International folkloristics: Classic contributions by the founders of folklore.* Rowman & Littlefield.

Engstrom, E. (2017). *Feminism, gender, and politics in NBC's* Parks and Recreation. Peter Lang.

Femia, J. (2002). Hegemony and consciousness in the thought of Antonio Gramsci. In J. Martin (ed.), *Antonio Gramsci: Critical assessments of Leading Political Philosophers* (Vol. 2) (pp. 263–286). Routledge.

Femia, J. (2010). Gramsci, Antonio (1891–1937). In M. Bevir (ed.), *Encyclopedia of Political Theory* (pp. 568–571). Sage.

Fenwick, B. (2020, August 23). The massacre that destroyed Tulsa's 'Black Wall Street.' *The New York Times.* https://www.nytimes.com/2020/07/13/us/tulsa-massacre-graves-excavation.html

Filippini, M. (2017). *Using Gramsci: A New Approach* (D. J. Barr, Trans.). Pluto Press.

Fischman, G., & McLaren, P. (2005). Rethinking critical pedagogy and the Gramscian and Freirean legacies: From organic to committed intellectuals or critical pedagogy, commitment, and praxis. *Cultural Studies↔Critical Methodologies, 5,* 425–446.

Fixmer-Oraiz, N., & Wood, J. (2019). *Gendered lives* (13th ed.). Cengage.

Forgacs, D. (2016). Gramsci undisabled. *Modern Italy, 21,* 345–360.

Forgacs, D. (ed.). (2000). *The Antonio Gramsci reader.* NYU Press.

Galician, M.-L. (2019). *Sex, love, and romance in the Mass Media: Analysis and criticism of Unrealistic Portrayals and Their Influence.* Kendall Hunt.

Garcia, V. (1992). Gramsci, women and the state. *Alternate Routes, 9,* 1–25.

Gencarella, S. (2010). Gramsci, good sense, and critical folklore studies. *Journal of Folklore Research, 47,* 221–252.

Gideonse, T. (2019, May 29). The cultural universals in *Avengers: Endgame. Anthropology News.* http://www.anthropology-news.org/index.php/2019/05/29/the-cultural-universals-in-avengers-endgame/

Gillam, K., & Wooden, S. (2008). Post-princess models of gender: The new man and Disney/Pixar. *Journal of Popular Film and Television, 36,* 2–8.

Giroux. H. (1997). *Pedagogy and the politics of hope: Theory, culture and schooling.* Westview Press.

Gitlin, T. (1980). *The Whole World is watching: Mass media in the making and unmaking of the New Left.* University of California Press.

Gitlin, T. (1987). Television's screens: Hegemony in transition. In D. Lazere (ed.), *American media and Mass Culture* (pp. 240–265). University of California Press.

Gottdiener, M. (1985). Hegemony and mass culture: A semiotic approach. *American Journal of Sociology, 90,* 979–1001.

Gramsci, A. (1971). *Selections from the Prison Notebooks.* (Q. Hoare & G. Nowell Smith, Trans. & eds.). International Publishers.

Gramsci, A. (1992). *Prison notebooks Vol. 1.* Columbia University Press.

Gramsci, A. (1999). *Selections from the Prison Notebooks of Antonio Gramsci.* (Q. Hoare & G. Nowell Smith, Trans. & eds.). ElecBook. (Original work published 1971)

Gramsci, A. (2000). *The Antonio Gramsci reader: Selected writings, 1916–1935.* (D. Forgacs, ed.). New York University Press.

Gramsci, A. (2012). *Selections from Cultural Writings.* Haymarket Books.

Hall, S. (1977). Culture, the media, and the 'ideological effect.' In J. Curran, M. Gurevitch, & J. Wollacott (eds.), *Mass communication and society* (pp. 315–348). Edward Arnold.

Hall, S. (1980) Encoding/decoding. In S. Hall, D. Hobson, A. Love, & P. Willis (eds.), *Culture, media, language* (pp. 128–38). Hutchinson.

Hall, S. (1986). Gramsci's relevance for the study of race and ethnicity. *Journal of Communication Inquiry, 10*(5), 5–27.

Hall, S. (2019). Encoding and decoding in the television discourse. In D. Morley (ed.), *Essential essays, volume 1.* (pp. 257–276). Duke University Press. (Original work published 1973; republished 2007)

Hall, S., & Whannell, P. (1963). *The Popular Arts.* Pantheon.

Hardt, H. (1992). *Critical Communication Studies: Communication, history, and theory in America.* Routledge.

Harris, D. (2015). Hegemony and the media. In G. Ritzer (ed.), *The Blackwell encyclopedia of sociology* (pp. 1–4). John Wiley & Sons.

Harrison, S., Carlsen, A., & Skerlavaj, M. (2019, July-August). Marvel's blockbuster machine. *Harvard Business Review.* https://hbr.org/2019/07/marvels-blockbuster-machine

Hartson, M. (2016). The Bourne refusal: Changing the rules of the game? In E. Abele & J. A. Gronbeck-Tedesco (eds.), *Screening images of American masculinity in the age of postfeminism* (pp. 51–68). Lexington.

Herman, E., & Chomsky, N. (1988). *Manufacturing consent: The Political Economy of the mass media.* Pantheon.

Hirschhorn, T. (2015). Gramsci monument. *Rethinking Marxism, 27,* 213–240.

Hoare, G., & Sperber, N. (2016). *An introduction to Antonio Gramsci: His life, thought and legacy.* Bloomsbury.

Hobsbawm, E. J. (1982). Gramsci and Marxist political theory. In A. S. Sassoon (ed.), *Approaches to Gramsci* (pp. 20–69). Writers and Readers Publishing Cooperative Society.

Hodge, J. (2018, May 3). Why superhero films such as Infinity War aren't ruining cinema (or our minds). *The Conversation.* https://theconversation.com/why-superhero-films-such-as-infinity-war-arent-ruining-cinema-or-our-minds-95864

Hofstede, G. (1980). *Culture's consequences: International differences in Work Related Values.* Sage.

Hoggart, R. (1957). *The uses of literacy: Aspects of working Class Life.* Chatto.

Holub, R. (1992). *Antonio Gramsci: Beyond Marxism and postmodernism.* Routledge.

Holub, R. (2010). Towards a global space of democratic rights: On Benjamin, Gramsci, and Polanyi. In A. Pusca (ed.), *Walter Benjamin and the aesthetics of change* (pp. 10–54). Palgrave.

Howarth, D. (2015). Gramsci, hegemony and post-Marxism. In M. McNally (ed.), *Antonio Gramsci* (pp. 195–213). Palgrave Macmillan.

Jackson, D., Engstrom, E., & Emmers-Sommer, T. (2007). Think leader, think male *and* female: Sex vs. seating arrangement as leadership cues. *Sex Roles: A Journal of Research, 57,* 713–723.

Jacques, C., Islar, M., & Lord, G. (2019). Post-truth: Hegemony on social media and implications for sustainability communication. *Sustainability, 11*(7), 2120.

Jandt, F. E. (2013). *An introduction to Intercultural Communication: Identities in a Global Community.* Sage.

Johnson, A. (1997). *The Gender Knot: Unraveling Our Patriarchal Legacy.* Temple University Press.

Johnson, K. (2013, July 26). A summer place in the South Bronx. *The New York Times,* p. C19.

Jones, M. (2017, August 3). The fragile masculinity of the MCU (or why Captain America shouldn't be afraid to cry). */Film.* https://www.slashfilm.com/the-fragile -masculinity-of-the-mcu/

Jones, S. (2006). *Antonio Gramsci.* Routledge.

Kang, I. (2019, April 26). The worst scene in *Endgame* is the one that's supposed to be the most feminist. *Slate.* https://slate.com/culture/2019/04/avengers-endgame -female-representation-black-widow.html

Katz, J. (2020, May 19). Donald Trump and the tragedy of failed 'masculine' leadership. *Ms.* https://msmagazine.com/2020/05/19/donald-trump-and-the-tragedy-of -failed-masculine-leadership/?

Katz, J. (Writer), & Earp, J. (Director). (2013). *Tough guise 2: Violence, manhood, and American culture* [Video documentary]. Northhampton, MA: Media Education Foundation.

Kenway, J. (2001). Remembering and regenerating Gramsci. In K. Weiler (ed.), *Feminist engagements* (pp. 47–65). Routledge.

Kellner, D. (2009). Media industries, political economy, and media/cultural studies. In J. Holt & A. Perren (eds.), *Media industries: History, theory, and method* (pp. 95–107). Wiley-Blackwell.

Knapp, M., & Hall, J. (2009). *Nonverbal communication in Human Interaction* (7th ed.). Cengage.

Landy, M. (1986). Culture and politics in the work of Antonio Gramsci. *boundary 2, 14*(3), 49–70.

Landy, M. (1994). *Film, politics, and Gramsci.* University of Minnesota Press.

Landy, M. (2008). Gramsci, passive revolution, and media. *boundary 2, 35*(3), 99–131.

Lather, P. (1984). Critical theory, curricular transformation and feminist mainstreaming. *Journal of Education, 166,* 49–62.

Lawless, J., & Fox, R. (2004). *Why don't women run for office?* [Policy report]. Brown University Taubman Center for Public Policy.

Leadbeater, C. (2004) *The Pro-Am revolution: How enthusiasts are changing our society and economy.* https://charlesleadbeater.net/2004/11/the-pro-am -revolution/

Lears, T. J. (1985). The concept of cultural hegemony: Problems and possibilities. *American Historical Review, 90*(3), 567–593.

Ledwith, M. (2009). Antonio Gramsci and feminism: The elusive nature of power. *Educational Philosophy and Theory, 41*, 684–697.

Levant, R. (2011). Research in the psychology of men and masculinity: Using the gender role strain paradigm as a framework. *American Psychologist, 66*, 765–776.

Lewis, C. (1992). Making sense of common sense: A framework for tracking hegemony. *Critical Studies in Mass Communication, 9*, 277–292.

Liguori, G. (2015). Conceptions of subalternity in Gramsci. In M. McNally (ed.), *Antonio Gramsci* (pp. 118–133). Palgrave Macmillan.

Livingston, G., & Parker, K. (2019, June 12). 8 facts about American dads. *FactTank.* https://www.pewresearch.org/fact-tank/2019/06/12/fathers-day-facts/

Madigan, T. (2001). *The burning: Massacre, destruction, and the Tulsa Race Riot of 1921.* Thomas Dunne Books.

Martin, J. (1997). Hegemony and the crisis of legitimacy in Gramsci. *History of the Human Sciences, 10*, 37–56.

Martin, J. (ed.). (2002). *Antonio Gramsci: Critical assessments of Leading Political Philosophers* (Vol. 1). Routledge.

Martin, J. (2015). Morbid symptoms: Gramsci and the crisis of liberation. In M. McNally (ed.), *Antonio Gramsci* (pp. 34–51). Palgrave Macmillan.

Marzani, C. (Trans.). (1957). *The open Marxism of Antonio Gramsci.* Cameron Associates.

Mayo, P. (2014). Gramsci and the politics of education. *Capital & Class, 38*(2), 385–398.

Mayo, P. (2017). Gramsci, hegemony and educational politics. In N. Pizzolato & J. D. Holst (eds.), *Antonio Gramsci: A pedagogy to change the world* (pp. 35–47). Springer.

McAdams, D. P. (2011). Narrative identity. In S. J. Schwartz, K. Luyckx, & V. L. Vignoles (eds.), *Handbook of identity theory and research* (pp. 99–115). Springer.

McCarthy, T. (2019, April 23). *Avengers: Endgame*: Film review. *Hollywood Reporter.* https://www.hollywoodreporter.com/review/avengers-endgame-review-1203971

McGrath, D. (2016). Some assembly required: Joss Whedon's bridging of masculinities in Marvel Films' *The Avengers*. In E. Abele & J. Gronbeck-Tedesco (eds.), *Screening images of American masculinity in the age of postfeminism* (pp. 135–151). Lexington.

McNally, M. (ed.) (2015). *Antonio Gramsci.* Palgrave Macmillan.

McSweeney, T. (2018). *Avengers assemble! Critical perspectives on the Marvel Cinematic Universe.* Columbia University Press.

Mercer, C. (1979). Culture and ideology in Gramsci. *Red Letters, 8*(19), 19–40.

Messerschmidt, J. W. (2018). *Hegemonic masculinity: Formulation, reformulation, and amplification.* Rowman & Littlefield.

Meyrowitz, J. (1985). *No sense of place.* Oxford University Press.

Mohan, M. (2019, May 27). *Avengers: Endgame*—Captain America, friendship, and masculinity. *Women Write about Comics*. https://womenwriteaboutcomics.com /2019/05/avengers-endgame-captain-america-friendships/

Molintas, D. (2020). *Shattering the glass: Will Gen Z bring us closer to gender equality in US hospitality leadership?* [Unpublished doctoral dissertation]. University of Nevada, Las Vegas.

Mouffe, C. (2002). Hegemony and ideology in Gramsci. In J. Martin (ed.), *Antonio Gramsci: Critical assessments of Leading Political Philosophers* (Vol. 2) (pp. 287–318). Routledge.

Mumby, D. (1997). The problem of hegemony: Rereading Gramsci for organizational communication studies. *Western Journal of Communication, 61*, 343–375.

Mulvey, L. (1975). Visual pleasure and narrative cinema. *Screen, 16*(3), 6–18.

NAMLE (n.d.). *A parent's guide to media literacy.* https://namle.net/a-parents-guide -to-media-literacy/

Natharius, D. (2004). The more we know the more we see. *American Behavioral Scientist, 48*, 238–247.

NJCASA (2019, October 2). Breaking down the boys' club. https://njcasa.org/news/ patriarchy-smash-avengers-part2/

Nichols, B. (2010). *Introduction to documentary* (2nd ed.). University of Indiana Press.

Ordoña, M. (2019, October 29). If comic-book movies aren't emotional and psychological cinema, why are we crying? *The Los Angeles Times.* https://www.latimes.com/entertainment-arts/movies/story/2019-10-29/comic-book-movies-joker -avengers-endgame-black-panther-scorsese-mcu

Pagano. R. (2017). Culture, education, and political leadership in Gramsci's thought. In N. Pizzolato & J. Holst, J. (eds.). *Antonio Gramsci: A pedagogy to Change the world* (pp. 49–66). Springer.

Parks and Recreation. (2012). Peabody Awards: Winners. http://peabodyawards .com/

Peters, M. A. (2007). Kinds of thinking, styles of reasoning. *Educational Philosophy and Theory, 39*, 350–363.

Pizzolato, N., & Holst, J. (eds.). (2017). *Antonio Gramsci: A pedagogy to change the world.* Springer.

Racine, L. (2009). Applying Antonio Gramsci's philosophy to postcolonial feminist social and political activism in nursing. *Nursing Philosophy, 10*, 180–190.

Reed, J. (2012). Theorist of subaltern subjectivity: Antonio Gramsci, popular beliefs, political passion, and reciprocal learning. *Critical Sociology, 39*, 561–591.

Rehling, N. (2009). *Extra-Ordinary Men: White Heterosexual Masculinity in contemporary Popular Cinema.* Lexington.

Reinhard, C. D., & Olson C. J. (2018) The superhero genre in film. In A. Geimer et al. (eds.), *Handbuch Filmsoziologie.* Springer Reference Sozialwissenschaften.

Rodriguez, A. M. (2018). The role of the Hollywood motion picture production code (1930-1966) in the creation of hegemony. In S. Coban (ed.), *Media, ideology and hegemony* (pp. 248–266). Brill.

Rao, S. (2019, April 30). This *Avengers: Endgame* battle scene captures Marvel's tricky relationship with female heroes. *The Washington Post*. https://www .washingtonpost.com/arts-entertainment/2019/04/30/this-avengers-endgame-battle -scene-captures-marvels-tricky-relationship-with-female-heroes/

Rojas, D. (2019, July 2). Unplugged: patriarchy smash with the Avengers—Part 1: Masculinity, trauma, and grief. *NJ Coalition Against Sexual Assault*. https://njcasa .org/news/patriarchy-smash-avengers-part1/

Rosengarten, F. (n.d.). *An introduction to Gramsci's life and thought*. www.marxists .org/archive/gramsci/intro.htm

Roublou, Y. (2012). 'Complex masculinities': The superhero in modern American movies. *Culture, Society & Masculinities*, *4*(1), 76–91.

Rowe, D. (2004). Antonio Gramsci: Sport, hegemony and the national-popular. In R. Guilianotti (ed.), *Sport and modern social theorists* (pp. 97–110). Palgrave Macmillan.

Rushkoff, D. (2010). *Program or be programmed: 10 Commandments for the Digital Age*. OR Books.

Schwarzmantel, J. J. (2014). *The Routledge guidebook to Gramsci's* Prison Notebooks. Routledge.

Santucci, A. (2010). *Antonio Gramsci* (G. Di Mauro with S. E. Di Mauro, Trans.). Monthly Review Press. (Original work published 2005)

Sassoon, A. S. (ed.). (1982). *Approaches to Gramsci*. Writers and Readers Publishing Cooperative Society.

Sassoon, A. S. (ed.). (1987). *Women and the state: The Shifting Boundaries of public and private*. Routledge.

Savyasachi, B. (2019, May 3). A feminist review of *Avengers: Endgame*: A soft nod to female solidarity. *Feminism in India*. https://feminisminindia.com/2019/05/03/ avengers-endgame-feminist-review/

Scharrer, E. (2001). Tough guys: The portrayal of hypermasculinity and aggression in televised police dramas. *Journal of Broadcasting & Electronic Media*, *45*, 615–634.

Schwarzmantel, J. J. (2014). *The Routledge guidebook to Gramsci's* Prison Notebooks. Routledge.

Scorsese, M. (2019, November 4). Martin Scorsese: I said Marvel movies aren't cinema. Let me explain. *The New York Times*. https://www.nytimes.com/2019/11/04/ opinion/martin-scorsese-marvel.html

Siede, C. (2019, April 29). *Avengers: Endgame* doesn't earn its big 'girl power' moment. *AV Club*. https://film.avclub.com/avengers-endgame-doesn-t-earn-its-big -girl-powermom-1834366317

Simon, J. (2013). Locating gender and resistance through a feminist application of Gramsci's 'organic intellectual': An analysis of *Time Magazine*'s 2002 'Person of the Year.' *Southern Communication Journal*, *1*, 56–69.

Slaughter, J. (2011). Gramsci's place in women's history. *Journal of Modern Italian Studies*, *16*, 256–272.

Soldier Blue. [Review]. (n.d.). *Time Out*. https://www.timeout.com/movies/soldier -blue

Sonnad, N. (2016, December 7). Data scientist Cathy O'Neil on the cold destructiveness of big data. *Quartz.* https://qz.com/819245/data-scientist-cathy-oneil-on-the-cold-destructiveness-of-big-data/

Steele, T. (1997). *The emergence of Cultural Studies 1945-65.* Lawrence and Wishart.

Storey, J. (2009). *Cultural theory and Popular Culture* (5th ed.). Pearson.

Taylor, D. J. (2017, June 16–27). Entertaining the masses. *The New Statesman*, pp. 52–53.

The 1619 project. (2019, August 18). *The New York Times Magazine.* https://www.nytimes.com/interactive/2019/08/14/magazine/1619-america-slavery.html

Thomas, P. D. (2009). *Gramscian moment: Philosophy, hegemony and Marxism.* Brill.

Thompson, E. P. (1963). *The making of the English Working Class.* Victor Gollancz.

Trepanier, R. (1991). *Towards an Alternative Media Strategy: Gramsci's theory in practice.* Unpublished master's thesis. National Library of Canada.

Trujillo, N. (1991). Hegemonic masculinity on the mound: Media representations of Nolan Ryan and American sports culture. *Critical Studies in Media Communication, 8,* 290–308.

Tyler, A. (2019, December 26). MCU theory: The sad reason behind Captain America's Endgame support group. *Screen Rant.* https://screenrant.com/mcu-avengers-endgame-captain-america-falcon-therapy-theory/

UNESCO (2005). *The 2005 convention on the protection and promotion of the diversity of cultural expressions.* https://en.unesco.org/creativity/sites/creativity/files/passeport-convention2005-web2.pdf

Ussher, J. M. (1997). *Fantasies of femininity: Reframing the boundaries of sex.* Rutgers University Press.

Vavrus, M. D. (2002). Domesticatory patriarchy: Hegemonic masculinity & television's 'Mr. Mom.' *Critical Studies in Media Communication, 19,* 352-375.

Valian, V. (1999). *Why So Slow? The advancement of women.* MIT Press.

Yahr, E. (2015, February 24). Why we'll never see another show like *Parks and Recreation* again. *The Washington Post.* https://www.washingtonpost.com/news/arts-and-entertainment/wp/2015/02/24/why-well-never-see-another-show-like-parks-and-recreation-again/

Wade, L., & Bridges, T. (2020, May 13). Why we need a 'feminine' economic reopening. *Gender & Society.* https://gendersociety.wordpress.com/2020/05/13/why-we-need-a-feminine-economic-reopening/

Watercutter, A. (2019, March 11). Captain Marvel is about female power—not empowerment. *Culture.* https://www.wired.com/story/captain-marvel-is-about-female-power-not-empowerment/

White, M. (2019, May 20). *Avengers: Endgame*: Male entitlement undermines Steve Rogers' core characteristics and story arc. *Cinemalogue.* http://cinemalogue.com/2019/05/20/avengers-endgame-male-entitlement-undermines-steve-rogers-core-characterization-and-story-arc/

Williams, R. (1961). *The Long Revolution.* Chatto & Windus.

Williams, R. (1977). *Marxism and literature.* Oxford University Press.

Williams, G. (2002). The concept of *egemonia* in the thought of Antonio Gramsci. In J. Martin (ed.), *Antonio Gramsci: Critical assessments of Leading Political Philosophers* (Vol. 2) (pp. 229–224). Routledge.

Wooden, S. R., & Gillam, K. (2014). *Pixar's Boy Stories: Masculinity in a Postmodern Age.* Rowman & Littlefield.

Zimmerman, J. (2005). *Whose America? Culture wars in the Public Schools.* Harvard University Press.

Zinn, H. (1980*). A People's History of the United States.* Harper & Row.

Zompetti, J. (1997). Toward a Gramscian critical rhetoric. *Western Journal of Communication, 61*(1), 66–86.

Zompetti, J. (2012). The cultural and communicative dynamics of capital: Gramsci and the impetus for social action. *Culture, Theory and Critique, 53*, 365–382.

Index

access: to education, 118; power sacrificed for, 34–35
Acu, A., 87
African Americans, 56–57, 62–63
Agresta, M., 55–56
algorithms, 116
Althusser, Louis, 35
Anthony, N., 94, 95
Apple, M. W., 10
Arellano, L., 75
Arnot, M., 68
L'Arroseur arose (Lumiere Brothers), 52
Artz, B. L., 15, 62–63
Asher-Perrin, E., 77
Askew, Rilla, 58
Atkinson, J., 75
authorship, 29, 39
The Avengers (Whedon), 80–81
Avengers: Endgame (Russo and Russo): assessment of, 97–103; box-office success of, 82, 97; emotional expressiveness, 89, 90–93, 98–99; family emphasis and fatherhood, 95–97, 100; fear, self-doubt, and vulnerability expressions, 93–95, 99–100; giving and asking for help, 88–90, 98; hegemonic masculinity and Marvel's new man, 87–88;

plot summary, 85–87; women and traditional/hegemonic femininity, 103–7

Baldwin, James, 56–57
Bates, T., 17
Berk, R., 30
Birmingham University Centre for Contemporary Cultural Studies (BCCCS), 37–38
Blanche, Alice Guy, 53
Blumberg, A. T., 87
Boon, K., 70, 72
Bourdieu, Pierre, 39–41
Bourne film franchise, 76
Bové, P., 21
Bridges, T., 71
Briziarelli, M., 14, 25n8
Brueggeman, N., 59
Brusuelas, C., 94, 100, 104
Burbules, N. C., 30
Buttigieg, J., 6–7, 111

Calafell, B., 75
capitalism: critical media literacy and, 47; disruption avoided in, 114; education and, 117, 118; folklore and, 66; Fordism and "Hollywoodism," 52; global media

133

market and, 113; in Gramsci's thought, 6–8, 14; Hollywood power structure and, 108; journalism and, 44–45; mass media and, 15; profit, need for, 97; transnational organizations and, 32

Captain America: The Winter Soldier (Russo and Russo), 109n2

Captain Marvel (Boden and Fleck), 105

Carlson, G. M., 88

Carragee, K. M., 20, 25n12

Chomsky, Noam, 43–44

civil society: common sense and negotiation of, 32–34; folklore and, 51; hegemony and, 8–13; mass media and, 15

clickbait, 35

Clinton, Hillary, 107

common sense: civil society and, 32; critical awareness and, 17; documentary and, 45, 46; folklore and, 45–46; good sense *vs.,* 12, 38, 46, 54; Gramsci on, 11–12; journalism and, 44; new, 112–13; philosophy of praxis and, 42; scientific evidence and, 33; social media and, 32–33

Comolli, J.-L., 97, 98

Connell, Raewyn (R. W.), 69–71, 73, 75, 83n2, 101, 102, 107

consent, 8–9, 34–35

content and form, 28, 64–65

convention in filmmaking, 52–54

"Convention on the Protection and Promotion of the Diversity of Cultural Expression" (UNESCO), 63

counterhegemony: corporate dismantling of the anti-hegemonic, 112; *Endgame* and, 100; future research, 108; gender and, 76–78, 81–82; Gramsci's theorization of, 12–13; moral and intellectual leadership and, 117; visual media and, 62–63

critical awareness: film spectatorship and, 56–57; folklore knowledge and, 50–51; Gramsci on, 16–19; misunderstanding the critique, 113–14; voting with economic resources, 112

critical media literacy, 30–31, 35. *See also* media literacy

critical thinking, 13, 30, 87

cultural production: cultural power and, 22; digital, access to, 114–15; *Endgame* and, 97; hegemony and, 10, 67–68; intellectuals and, 17–18; production of ideas, control over, 9

cultural studies, 20, 36–42

culture: hegemony and, 9–11; "new," struggle for, 64–65; reproduced in education, 31; as site of ideological struggle, 10. *See also* popular culture

Daddy Day Care (Carr), 75

Day, R., 10

De Beukelaer, C., 63

Debruge, P., 87, 100

Deer, C., 40

Dexter (Showtime), 75

digital media, 63–64, 114–17

Disney, 78–79, 109

documentary media, 44–45, 46

Dombroski, R., 14, 18, 67

dominance and hegemony, 8–9, 24n3

domination *vs.* hegemony, 8, 31–32

doxa, 39–40

Dundes, A., 50

education: access to, 118; civics, patriotic, 66; dynamic between student and teacher, 117; Gramsci on, 16–18; hegemony and, 10–11; indoctrination *vs.,* 27; intellectuals and teachers, relationship between, 38–39; MCU and, 87; media literacy and, 35–36; media literacy education, 28–30; praxis, philosophy of, 42;

textbook content battle, 55. *See also*
media literacy
emic, 40
Endgame. See Avengers: Endgame
etic, 40
European Union (EU), 32

false information, 116
La fée aux choux (Blanche), 53
Femia, J., 7–8, 12, 14, 17–18
femininity, hegemonic, 73
Feminist Frequency, 118
Fenwick, B., 61–62
film. *See* Hollywood, film and
television; *specific films by title*
Firefly (Fox), 76–77
folklore: common sense and, 45–46;
film and, 53–54; historical
representation and, 59–60; popular
culture and, 65–66; subaltern groups
and folkloric knowledge, 50–52
force and consent, balance between,
34–35
Fordism, 52
Forgacs, D., 4, 23n1, 25n10
form and content, 28, 64–65

Galician, Mary-Lou, 102
gaze, male, 92–93
Gencarella, S., 51
gender and gender ideology:
democratization of gender
relations, 102–3; Gramsci on, 68;
hegemonic femininity, 73; male
gaze, 92–93; "new man" persona
and counterhegemonic masculinity,
76–78; normative male alexithymia
hypothesis, 72, 83n3; rape culture
norms, defiance against, 102;
socialization and, 68, 69, 71–72,
83n3, 90, 118; traditional/hegemonic
femininity, 103–7. *See also*
Avengers: Endgame; masculinity,
hegemonic

genres, development of, 53–54
Gideonse, T., 87
Gillam, K., 70, 78–79, 98, 109
Giroux, H., 38–39
Gitlin, T., 9, 15, 18, 68
good sense, 12, 38, 46, 54
Gottdiener, M., 54
Gramsci, Antonio: about, 1, 3–8;
on cinema *vs.* theatre, 64–65; on
critical awareness, education, and
intellectuals, 16–19; on gender
ideology, 68; hegemony theory, 8–
13; on mass communication, 13–15;
media literacy, influence on, 31–35;
The Prison Notebooks, 6–7. *See also*
hegemony; media literacy
Gramscian studies, 23n1
The Great Hack (Netflix), 46
"The Great Train Robbery" (Porter), 53
Guillem, S. M., 25n8

Hall, Stuart, 20, 24n2, 37–38, 41
Hamlet (Shakespeare), 19
Hardt, Hanno, 61
Harris, D., 18, 24n5
Hartson, M., 76
hegemonic masculinity. *See* masculinity,
hegemonic
hegemony: action and meaning,
combination of, 28; definitions of,
1–2, 7–8; determinism and, 54;
Hollywood conventions and, 52–54;
ideology, relationship with, 41; mass
media and, 13–15; as mediator, 34;
origins of term, 24n2; propaganda
model and, 43–44; theory of, 8–13;
in visual media, 62–65; wholeness in
process of, 31–32
Here and Now (NPR), 113–14
Herman, Edward S., 43–44
Hirshhorn, Thomas, 24n1
historical representation in film, 54–60,
61–62
Hodge, J., 87

Hoggart, Richard, 37
Hollywood, film and television:
    alternative discourses and
    collaboration, 61; convention
    and, 52–54; folklore and, 50–52,
    53–54, 65–66; Gramsci on cinema
    vs. theatre, 64–65; hegemony in
    visual media, 62–65; historical
    representation and massacres, 54–60;
    legacy–digital transformations and,
    49, 63–65; organic intellectual
    activity and, 60–62; power structure
    of Hollywood, 108; Western films,
    55–57
Holst, J., 16
Holub, R., 5–6, 10, 51

"I agree" buttons, 35
ideas and civil society, 9–10
identity-construction, 50, 53–54, 66
ideologies: action and meaning,
    combination of, 28; culture as site
    of struggle over, 10; hegemony,
    relationship with, 41; mass media
    and, 14; in popular culture, 16. *See
    also* gender and gender ideology;
    hegemony
intellectuals: film, television, and,
    60–62; Gramsci on, 17–18, 38–39;
    organic, 18, 39, 50, 60–62; teachers,
    relationship with, 38–39

Jones, S., 87, 95, 103
journalism: documentary films,
    44–45; Gramsci and, 5, 14, 42–43;
    propaganda model, 43–45

Kang, I., 104
Karikari, E., 14
Katz, Jackson, 70–72
Kellner, D., 15, 20–21
Kenway, J., 71, 73
"Key Questions When Analyzing Media
    Messages" (NAMLE), 29–30

knowledge: anti-hegemonic, 60;
    folkloric, 50–51; official, 10

Landy, M., 14, 18, 21, 25n9, 25n12, 45
language: intellectuals and, 38; power
    imbalances and, 41–42, 47
Leadbeater, C., 115
Ledwith, M., 68
Levant, Ronald F., 72–73, 81, 83n3
Lewis, C., 8
Liguori, G., 68
The Lone Ranger (Verbinsky), 55–56
Lovecraft Country (HBO), 58–60, 61,
    111
Lumiere Brothers, 52

Madigan, Tim, 58
*The Making of the English Working
    Class* (Thompson), 36–37
male gaze, 92–93
Martin, J., 4–9
Marvel Cinematic Universe (MCU),
    78–81, 109. *See also Avengers:
    Endgame*
Marzani, C., 3
masculinity, hegemonic: concept of, 69–
    73, 83n2; gender ideology and, 68;
    mediated, 74–79; in superhero genre
    and Marvel Cinematic Universe
    (MCU), 78–82. *See also Avengers:
    Endgame*; new man persona, Pixar
massacres, representation of, 57–60
mass media: capitalism and, 15;
    hegemony and, 13–15; Hoggart on
    massification, 37; ideology conveyed
    by, 10; masculinity and, 70. *See also*
    digital media
Mayo, P., 41–42
McGrath, D., 80–81
McSweeney, T., 79–80
media literacy: cultural turn and,
    39–42; defined, 2; digital and social
    media and, 114–17; folklore and
    common sense, 45–46; "goes without

saying," 40; Gramscian influence on, 31–35; intellectuals and teachers, relationship between, 38–39; journalism, news, and propaganda, 42–45; key questions and critical media literacy in education, 28–31; popular culture texts taken seriously in, 66; "reading too much into it," 33; transformations of, 35–38. *See also* critical awareness; education
Melies, Georges, 53
Mercer, C., 10
Messerschmidt, J. W., 70, 102
misinformation, 116
Mohan, M., 99
Mosley, Tonya, 113
Mouffe, C., 13
Mulvey, Laura, 92
Mumby, D., 8
Murphy, B. O., 62–63
Mussolini, Benito, 4, 5
My Lai Massacre (1968), 57, 60

Narboni, J., 97, 98
Natharius, D., 19, 112
National Association for Media Literacy Education (NAMLE), 29–30, 31, 48n1, 118
negotiation: common sense and, 32; cultural studies and, 20, 38; film and levels of, 52; folklore and, 51–52; innovation, appearance of, 47; organic intellectuals and, 39; representation and, 44, 54; small changes not disrupting hegemony, 114; transnational media and, 33; of values, in hegemonic process, 52
Nelson, Ralph, 57
New Jersey Coalition Against Sexual Assault (NJCASA), 101–2, 107–8
new man persona, *Avengers*. *See* *Avengers: Endgame*
new man persona, Pixar, 76–78, 98
news, corporate, 43–44

Nichols, B., 44
normalization, 9–11, 12
normative male alexithymia hypothesis, 72, 83n3, 88, 91, 94, 100

Obama, Barack, 107
Olson C. J., 79
O'Neill, Cathy, 116
Ordoña, M., 97–98
organic intellectuals, 18, 39, 50, 60–62

Parks and Recreation (NBC), 77–78
personal information, commodification of, 115–16
Peters, M. A., 30
philosophy and folkloric meaning, 51
Pierce, Wendell, 113
Pixar, 78, 98, 109
Pizzolato, N., 16
pleasure and media literacy, 33–35
police officers, representation of, 113–14
popular culture: *Avengers: Endgame* and, 82, 97, 101–2, 119n2; cultural studies and, 20; digital media and politics of, 114; documentary and, 45; folklore and, 65–66; gender and, 68–69; Gramscian cultural turn, 39–42; Gramsci on, 16, 119; Hollywoodism and, 52, 54; oppositional ideology and, 68; US world dominance in, 63; as view into culture, 107; Western genre and, 56–57
Porter, Edwin S., 53
power: conditions of, 41; corporate dismantling of the anti-hegemonic, 112; critical media literacy and, 30; disempowerment, 27, 51–52; distributed in cultural institutions, 32–33; domination *vs.* hegemony and, 8; empowerment, illusion of, 33; gender relations and, 68; regional language and, 41–42, 47; sacrificing,

for access, 34–35; struggle between scientific consensus and hegemonic power, 33
praxis, philosophy of, 42, 118
The Prison Notebooks (Gramsci), 6–7
"Pro-Am Revolution" in digital media, 115
production of ideas, control over, 9. *See also* cultural production
propaganda model, 43–45

race: hegemony in Black American culture, 62–63; Tulsa Race Massacre representation and, 57–60, 61–62; Western films and, 56–57
Racine, L., 25n8
Rao, S., 104
rape culture norms, defiance against, 102
Reed, J., 115
Rehling, N., 74
Reinhard, C. D., 79
representation: cultural turn and, 39; film and historical representation, 54–60, 61–62; negotiation and, 44, 54
reproduction, 10–11, 31, 52
Rodriguez, A. M., 25n12
Rojas, D., 89, 95, 101–2, 107–8
Roublou, Y., 79, 80
Rowe, D., 25n12
Rushkoff, D., 48n2
Russo, Joe, 109n4
Ryan, Nolan, 74

Sand Creek Massacre (1864), 57, 60
Santucci, A., 6
Sassoon, A. S., 12–13, 17
Scharrer, E., 75
Schuct, Tatiana, 6
Schur, Michael, 83n4
Schwarzmantel, J. J., 6–7
science, 33, 51
Scorsese, Martin, 97

semiotics, 2, 54
Serenity (Whedon), 76–77
1776 Commission, 66
Shakespeare, William, 19–20
Siede, C., 104
Simon, J., 25n12
"The 1619 Project" (*New York Times*), 66
Slaughter, J., 68
social change: behavior *vs.*, 75; common sense and, 17; counterhegemonies and process of, 12–13; education and, 6, 16–17; Gramsci on theatre and, 67–68; hegemony theory and, 12–13; Marvel's "new man" and, 82; resistance to, 7–8
socialization and gender, 68, 69, 71–72, 83n3, 90, 118
social media, 32–33, 114–17
Soldier Blue (Nelson), 57, 111
Sons of Anarchy (FX), 19
La Sortie de l'usine Lumiere a Lyon (Lumiere Brothers), 52
Star Wars film franchise, 75
the state and hegemony, 8–11
Steele, T., 36
Steiner, Linda, 12, 25n7
subaltern groups: cultural studies and, 38; folklore and, 45, 51; Gramsci's notion of, 28; regional language and, 47
superhero genre, 78–81, 87. *See also Avengers: Endgame*
Supernatural (CW), 77
surveillance, 93, 118
symbolic violence, 40–41

television. *See* Hollywood, film and television; *specific shows by title*
textbook content, battle over, 55
Thompson, E. P., 36–37
"A Trip to the Moon" (Melies), 53
Trujillo, N., 74
The Tulsa Lynching of 1921 (Cinemax), 58

Tulsa Race Massacre (1921), 57–60, 61–62

Uncle Tom's Cabin (Stowe), 59
The Uses of Literacy (Hoggart), 37
Ussher, J. M., 73

Vavrus, M. D., 74–75
violence, symbolic, 40–41

Wade, L., 71
Watchmen (HBO), 58, 60, 61, 111

Western film genre, 55–57
Whannell, Paddy, 20, 37
Whedon, Joss, 76–77
Williams, G., 12
Williams, Raymond, 31–32, 36, 37
The Wire (HBO), 113–14
Wooden, S. R., 70, 78–79, 98, 109
working-class life and culture, 36–37

Zimmerman, J., 55
Zinn, Howard, 60
Zompetti, J., 13, 19, 25n12

About the Authors

Erika Engstrom (PhD, University of Florida) is a professor and the director of the School of Journalism and Media at the University of Kentucky. Her research focuses on media portrayals of gender, love and romance, and religion. Her books include *The Bride Factory: Mass Media Portrayals of Women and Weddings* and *Feminism, Gender, and Politics in NBC's* Parks and Recreation.

Ralph Beliveau is an associate professor in the Creative Media Production area of the Gaylord College of Journalism and Mass Communication at the University of Oklahoma and affiliate faculty in Film and Media Studies and Women's and Gender Studies. He writes and teaches about media education and literacy, popular culture, and video production. He is the co-editor of *Screening #MeToo: Rape Culture in Hollywood*, contributing author of *Digital Literacy: A Primer on Media, Identity, and the Evolution of Teaching*, and co-editor of *International Horror Film Directors: Global Fear*.